A President Expresses Concern on a Visit to Westminster Abbey

Poet's Corner had no epitaph
to mark the Welshman's
sullen art or craft
because, they said,
his morals were below
the standards there.
I mentioned the ways of Poe
and Byron,
and the censored Joyce's works;
at least the newsmen listened,
noted my remarks
and his wife, Caitlin, wrote.
We launched a clumsy, weak campaign,
the bishops met
and listened to the lilting lines again.
Later, some Welshmen brought to me
a copy of the stone
that honors now the beauty he set free
from a godhead of his own.

From *There's Always A Reckoning*
by Jimmy Carter, 39th.President of the United States of America.

DYLAN THOMAS
AND
HIS WORLD

From a painting by Anthony James

DYLAN THOMAS AND HIS WORLD

by Derek Perkins

Photography by Len Pitson

Foreword by Jimmy Carter, 39th. President of the United States of America

DOMINO BOOKS (WALES) LTD

First published in 1995
by Domino Books (Wales) Ltd
P O Box 32 Swansea SA1 1FN

Tel. 01792 459378
Fax. 01792 466337

ISBN 1 85772 160 8 (paper)

1 85772 159 4 (cased)

FOREWORD

I am delighted to be able to introduce 'Dylan Thomas and His World', a book about the life and work of the most famous Welsh poet.

The book is an overview of Thomas's time in Swansea and emphasizes his Welsh upbringing. It places the poet in his local environment and its thesis is simple: one cannot understand Thomas the poet without reference to the area in which he lived, his childhood and where he grew up. For Thomas, West Wales in general and Swansea in particular were his world. This local knowledge is important in understanding his prose and especially his verse.

I have long been an admirer of the work of Dylan Thomas and have visited Swansea and Laugharne. I am especially pleased to write this foreword at a time when the City of Swansea celebrates the UK Year of Literature. The publication of the book is to coincide with this event and I wish it every success.

Jimmy Carter
39th. President
The United States of America

To Joan and Paul
who make everything worthwhile

INTRODUCTION

I make no excuses for adding to the growing volume of material on the life and work of the most famous of Welsh poets. The book examines the influences of Thomas's background on his work. Dylan Thomas loved Wales. He looked at its faults with a keen, derisory and sometimes cynical eye and loved the land of his birth all the more. To the young, the 'grass is always greener' in far away places and from time to time, Thomas escaped to explore the wider world. But it was in the people and the land of Wales that he found inspiration: it was here that he wrote his best work.

It is sometimes more difficult to be successful at home and Thomas's time in America was the start of international acclaim. There, not only was he well known as a writer but he also became famous as a reader and raconteur. It is true to say that the Americans understood that genius may be a little eccentric at times and he was invited back to the States several times. America and the Americans influenced him greatly.

In the writing of this book, I am indebted to many especially the late Constantine Fitzgibbon, Thomas's biographer, to Paul Ferris who wrote 'Dylan Thomas' in 1977 and Kent Thompson whose interviews are full of information about Thomas in Swansea. His unpublished Ph.D. Thesis on 'Dylan Thomas in Swansea' was especially helpful.

It is hoped that this slim volume will persuade the reader to seek out Thomas's work and read or better listen to it for its intrinsic beauty of sound, language and style. Also, it is hoped that the reader will seek out the places in South and West Wales that inspired Thomas, especially Swansea, the Mumbles, Gower, Laugharne and New Quay.

Derek Perkins

ACKNOWLEDGEMENTS

The publishers are grateful to the following:

Curtis Brown Group Ltd, agents for Paul Ferris for permission to use quotations from his book, *Dylan Thomas*.

Jimmy Carter, 39th. President of the United States of America.

Celtic Publications Ltd. (Swansea).

Celtic Educational Services Ltd. (Swansea).

Christopher Davies (Publishers), Swansea.

Cornell University Press, New York.

Emlyn Davies for the calligrams.

James A. Davies.

J. M. Dent & Sons Ltd.

Malcolm E. Gingerich.

David Higham Associates for permission to use quotations from Dylan Thomas's work including letters, stories and poetry.

Anthony James for his portrait of the young Dylan Thomas.

Librarian, University College of Swansea.

Len Pitson for the present-day photographs of Swansea, Gower and West Wales.

Bill Read.

Peter Stead.

Swansea City Council Archives Department for help with the 'old' Swansea photographs.

Dylan Thomas Society, Wales Branch.

Kent E. Thompson.

Weidenfeld & Nicholson.

CONTENTS

ILLUSTRATIONS

BEGINNINGS

In 1914, just before Dylan was born, Mr. and Mrs. Jack Thomas moved into 5 Cwmdonkin Drive, a stone's throw from the Uplands, a suburb of Swansea. Then, the Uplands was the fashionable place in which to live. Prosperous citizens, professional men and ambitious couples eagerly sought property in the area. Developers vied to build new homes and large detached and semi-detached houses began to replace the greenery. Streets like Mirador Crescent, Uplands Terrace, Richmond Terrace, the Grove and Cwmdonkin Drive grew apace. Those who lived elsewhere, in the centre of the town on its eastern edge for example, in Port Tennant, St. Thomas and Morriston, disliked the snobbishness of the Uplands clique: their pretensions, their affected language and high falutin' ways. They described those who lived in the Uplands and Sketty as having 'plus fours and no breakfast' or more crudely as having 'fur coats and no knickers'.

David John Thomas, Dylan's father, came from Johnstown, a village close to the country town of Carmarthen. He was the son of Ann and Evan Thomas, the latter known locally and affectionately as 'Thomas the Guard' because he worked for the railway. Evan was determined that his son, D J (called Jack) should have a good education and encouraged him to become a schoolmaster, a respected profession in those days. Jack became a pupil teacher in Carmarthen and won a scholarship to Aberystwyth University. In 1895, he graduated with a first class honours degree in English. He was fortunate to obtain a position at Swansea Grammar School and later became Senior English Master. He retired in December, 1937.

Dylan's mother, Florence, also came from West Wales. She was born about five miles from Carmarthen near the village of Llanybri, the youngest of seven children born to Anna and George Williams. The family moved to St. Thomas in Swansea where George also became a railway worker.

When Florence met Jack, she was working as a seamstress at a local drapery store. They were married on 30th. December, 1903 and their first child, Nancy, was born the following year.They first set up house in Sketty Avenue, then moved to Montpelier Street and eventually, when another child was expected, decided to buy a larger home: 5 Cwmdonkin Drive. Here Dylan Marlais Thomas was born on 27th. October, 1914.

The name 'Dylan' comes from *The Mabinogion,* a collection of medieval tales in Welsh. *'Verily,' said Math, concerning the fine yellow-haired boy, 'I will cause this one to be baptised and Dylan is the name I will give him.*[1] Dylan's middle name, 'Marlais,' also comes from his Welsh background and is a tribute to his paternal great-uncle, William Thomas, a poet who wrote under the bardic name of Gwilym Marles. Even at birth, Jack had hopes that his son would achieve literary fame.

The names were not given to the child without some misgivings. Florence was particularly worried about 'Dylan'. The Welsh pronunciation is 'Dullan' and she feared that his schoolmates would call him 'Dull One'. She need not have worried. He came to be known as 'Dillin'.[2]

Later, the poet explained in one of his letters to Pamela Hansford Johnson, *my unusual name - for some mad reason - comes from the 'Mabinogion'* ... [and] *rhymes with 'Chillun'.*[3]

GROWING UP IN SWANSEA

The Swansea Thomas knew was very different from today's modern city. He described it in his 'Reminscences of Childhood': *I was born in a large Welsh industrial town at the beginning of the Great War: an ugly, lovely town (or so it was, and is, to me), crawling, sprawling, slummed, unplanned jerry-villa'd and smug, suburbed by the side of a long and splendid-curving shore.*[4] The whole area was heavily industrialised with the preponderance of industry to the east of the town. There, the iron and tin-workers sweated before blazing furnaces and stevedores handled cargoes of coal and plate to and from Swansea docks. Young men were called up or volunteered to fight the Kaiser and as the war machine geared up for action the industrial heart of Swansea made bullets and shells for the men on the front line.

Horses were used to pull trams and buses and there were few cars. The roads outside the town were barely used except by horsemen and those walking to work. Radio and cinema were in their infancy, 'talkies' had just arrived, few people had telephones and, of course, there was no television. People with enough education could enjoy reading. A popular pastime was walking especially to the beaches (then unpolluted). Swansea beach with its yellow sand was a favourite. The train from Swansea to the Mumbles, then a small fishing village, was really a tram that followed the line of Swansea Bay and there were steam trains to places further afield like Porthcawl and Barry Island.

Churches and chapels were important influences in family life. Jack and Florence Thomas were not chapel-goers but their backgrounds meant they insisted that their children went. Before he was five, Thomas was sent to Walter Road Congregational Church and people recall that he looked 'like an angel'. Both father and son were steeped in the bible and in his writings, Thomas recalls the great stories he heard from the pulpit. He must have been taken occasionally to hear his Uncle David Rees preach at Paraclete Church in Newton. Thomas also went to stay with his aunt and uncle in the Mumbles for short holidays and was able to see how a parson spent his days with highlights on saints' days and Sundays.

Education was essential for those who wished to get on in life. There was a case for favouring English as the language of business and commerce and it was educational policy for Welsh to take a back seat in schools. Jack and Florence spoke Welsh but they largely ignored this heritage and their son spoke little of the language. Jack, however, had taught Welsh for extra income when the couple were first married. But his colleagues at the Grammar School never heard him speak the language in the day.

Most caring parents realised the importance of schooling, especially for boys, the future breadwinners for their families. At the age of seven, Thomas was sent to a private school run by a lady called Mrs Hole at her house in Mirador Crescent just down the hill from Cwmdonkin Drive. The school had two general teaching rooms and music lessons were given in a room upstairs. The fees were modest, a few pounds a term. The uniform was dark red and navy blue, and Thomas wore a cap, blazer and tie. Later, he reminisced about the establishment: *never was there such a dame school as ours, so firm and kind and smelling of galoshes, with the sweet and fumbled music of the piano lessons drifting down from the upstairs to the lonely schoolroom, where only the sometimes tearful wicked sat over undone sums, or to repeat a little crime - the pulling of a girl's hair during geography, the sly shin kick under the table during English literature. Behind the school was a narrow lane where only the oldest and boldest threw pebbles at windows, scuffled and boasted, fibbed about their relations ... and swapped gob-stoppers for slings, old knives for marbles, kite strings for foreign stamps. The lane was always the place to tell your secrets; if you did not have any, you invented them ... In the afternoons, when the children were good, they read aloud from Struwelpeter. And when they were bad, they sat alone in the empty classroom, hearing, from above them the distant, terrible, sad music of the late piano lessons.*[5]

Like most clever children, Dylan Thomas was mischievous but his shimmering curls and large brown eyes were appealing and teachers tended to spoil him. A number of incidents have been recorded.

Evelyn Burman Jones who attended the school at the same time, recalled when Thomas tugged her chair and she fell backwards knocking an aspidistra off a pedestal as she fell. Evelyn was blamed and not Thomas. On another occasion he fell in the lane and cut his knee on glass and claimed that Evelyn had pushed him. An amusing story concerned an end of term play. Taking the part of a colonel, Thomas had to carry a cane and then sit down and read a newspaper. Tired of hiding behind the paper, Dylan poked a hole in it and spat orange peel through it at the audience. He then rushed all over the stage, stabbing the air with the cane like a sword.[6] This brought the curtain down and the play was over.

Thomas had a very happy childhood. He told Margaret Taylor later, *There's only one thing that's worse than having an unhappy childhood, and that's having a too-happy childhood.*[7] Florence, his mother, doted on her boy. She loved to kiss and cuddle him and to provide treats. As Thomas was a sickly child, he often stayed home from school and was pampered in his bedroom. One of his favourite treats prepared by his mother was sugared bread and milk and even when he was grown up his wife was persuaded to give him the same meal. His mother did everything for him and was still removing the tops of his boiled eggs when he was seventeen. She defended him stoutly when he was in trouble and said he was not very strong. She often kept him from school sending notes to say he had anaemia, asthma, a heavy cold or some other unspecified illness. But his father influenced the growing boy more than his mother. It was D J who nurtured the boy's love for language and poetry and encouraged him to read and write. It was D J who persuaded him that there was something worthwhile in Shakespeare and verse. Thomas wrote to Pamela Hansford Johnson that D J was the broadest-minded man he had ever known and she soon realised that his father was his best friend. More than anything, Thomas respected his father.

The importance of Swansea in the development of the writer is clear from his work. Cwmdonkin Park is an example. He spent many happy hours in the Park as a child: *that small, interior world widened as I learned its names and its boundaries, as I discovered new refuges and ambushes in its miniature woods and jungles, hidden houses and lairs for the multitudes of the young, for cowboys and Indians.*[8] He remembered the games he used to play: *I carried a wooden rifle in Cwmdonkin Park and shot down the invisible unknown enemy like a flock of wild birds,*[9] and again, *the fountain basin where I sailed my ship.*[10]

In the autumn of 1925 shortly before he was eleven years old he went to Swansea Grammar School. There he met Daniel Jones who was to be one of his life-long friends. The poem, *The Hunchback in the Park* was, as his friend has pointed out, a recollection of the days they played in Cwmdonkin Park. There was a hunchback there, a man of no fixed abode, who stayed in the Park from the time it opened until it closed. Thomas and his friends saw him often for the Park was a favourite haunt for those playing truant from Swansea Grammar. It was in one sense on the way to the School for the 'old' Swansea Grammar on Mount Pleasant Hill could be approached from it via Terrace Road.

Down the hill from Thomas's house were the Grove and the Uplands. The young boy spent much of his time there. He had a sweet tooth and frequented Mrs. Ferguson's sweet shop in the Grove. A story is told that he asked for a bottle of lemonade and while Mrs. Ferguson went outside to get his 'pop' he took a handful of winegums from the jar on the counter.[11] Thomas loved winegums. It was in the Uplands too, that a cinema opened in 1933 (since then it has been a carpet warehouse and is now a branch of Lloyds Bank) and Thomas enjoyed going there. He impressed his close friends by collecting for Dr. Barnardo's and then breaking into the box to take them to the cinema where he puffed at Woodbines (a popular brand of cigarettes). Thomas also loved smoking.

Swansea Grammar School was already a well-established institution with a fine scholastic tradition when Thomas went there. The head, Trevor Owen, was a mild-mannered, caring man with a slight speech impediment who was popular with the 400 pupils and staff. Thomas was not scholastically inclined except for an all absorbing interest in English and English literature. He took part in most school events, however, and in 1926, for example, he won the Grammar School Mile: *the event of the afternoon was the winning of the mile (under 15 years) by D. M. Thomas. Because of his age and size he had a long start; he ran so well, however, that he was further ahead at the finish than he was at the start.*[12] Thomas was very proud of this success and kept a cutting in his wallet twenty-six years after the event. [13]

Thomas had a flare for English nurtured by his father and was co-editor of the *Grammar School Magazine* from December, 1929 to July, 1931. At a very early age he decided what he wanted to be. Whilst others wanted to be train drivers, solicitors, doctors or teachers, Thomas wanted to be a poet. He wanted to be a poet so much that it hurt. In his first term at school, he wrote *The Song of the Mischievous Dog* which was featured in the *School Magazine* and was his first published poem. He was so anxious to become a poet that he could not wait and it is clear that he plagiarised two poems. The first in 1927 was *His Requiem* actually written by Lilian Gard which appeared in the *Western Mail* and the other was *Sometimes* written by an American with a Welsh sounding name, Thomas S. Jones. While these poems were being 'stolen' Thomas was writing better work himself. The following is an extract from a poem which appeared in the *Western Mail* a month after *His Requiem.*

If the Gods had but given me one long day,
From fresh of the morning to starts at night,
With never a glance at the clock to say
The moments are slipping, farewells in sight.

He followed this when aged 13 by *Life Belt*, an early example of humorous verse and *Missing*, which is strong in rhythm and image. By the time he was fifteen, Thomas had a well-developed sense of criticism and a good idea of fine writing.

Outside school he continued his mischievous ways. Mervyn Levy, one of his school friends, recounts the following story: *My mother died when I was eight and after her death my father engaged a succession of nurses to look after his three children. One of these was a particularly comely and buxom girl whom Dylan and myself had long suspected of washing her breasts in the hand basin. The glass panels of the bathroom door were masked with variously coloured opaque paper, very thin and imparting to the top half of the door the aspect of a crude, stained-glass window. One day, in the holidays, we carefully scraped away two minute peepholes, one on either side, in readiness for the view that we dreamed would confirm our delicious suspicions. And so, not long afterwards, it turned out. Around three pm we crept up the sleepy, dark, afternoon stairs, and with an eye to our respective peepholes, beheld in ecstasy like two tiny elders, our own Susannah.*[14]

At school, Thomas was not much of a scholar, except at English, and life centred around the high jinks aimed at the masters. Bill Read mentions that these pranks were sometimes aimed at victimizing Thomas who was small, delicate and easily manoeuvred: *the bigger bully boys of the class would frequently grab him and stuff him, seat first, into the waste basket in such a way that he could not get out. It became the regular thing for the master to say as he entered the classroom 'Take Dylan out of the basket.'*[15]

There was some family concern that the young boy cared little for subjects other than English and English literature. Academically, at school, he was a failure. His mother recounted a conversation she had with her son: *I said, 'You know, you must try and get to the University - what are you going to do? Anybody'd think you were a Keats or something.' He looked at me - and he wasn't the cheeky type, he wasn't even a big talker - and he said, 'I'll be as good as Keats, if not better.'* [16]

When the Grammar School closed for the summer holidays on 31 July, 1931, it was the end of Thomas's school career. It was the time of the recession and jobs were scarce in Swansea and elsewhere. Out of a total population of 170,000 there were already nearly 10,000 unemployed. Thomas was fortunate to get a position with the *South Wales Daily Post* (later, the *South Wales Evening Post*) probably because of the influence of his father. He started as a copy-holder in the readers' room. but after a few months he was moved to the reporters' room and worked as a junior. Someone who worked with him at the time told me recently that he was not much of a reporter but spent much of his time in the taverns of Swansea. He described himself at this time as *A chap called Young Thomas. He worked on the 'Post' and used to wear an overcoat sometimes with the check lining inside out so that you could play giant draughts on him. He wore a conscious Woodbine too.*[17] Much of his spare time was spent in the back room of the Three Lamps (a Swansea pub), *I leant against the bar between an alderman and a solicitor, drinking bitter, wishing my father could see me ... He could not fail to see that I was a boy no longer, nor fail to be angry at the angle of my fag and my hat and the threat of the clutched tankard.* [18] There was no doubt that it was at this time that Thomas discovered his liking for the taverns of Swansea: he liked the convivial company at the bars and the conversation. He liked to talk and be listened to. He also liked beer. *I liked the taste of beer, its live, white lather, its brass-bright depth, the sudden world through the wet brown walls of the glass, the tilted rush to the lips and the slow swallowing down to the lapping belly, the salt on the tongue, the foam at the corners.*[19]

At this time Thomas made a number of contributions to local newspapers. Mainly factual, they consisted of accounts of the lives and work of local poets and of the visits of celebrities such as Landor, Borrow and Edward Thomas to Swansea. A good example of this prose work can be found in the *Herald of Wales* of 23 January, 1932. There, he wrote about Llewelyn Pritchard, the creator of Twm Siôn Cati, a popular figure in Welsh folklore: the story is full of garish interest and melodrama and ironically Thomas asserted: *No one can deny that the most attractive figures in literature are always those around whom a world of lies and legends has been woven ...* [20] By the time Thomas died in the 1950s this was true of him.

Swansea never failed to excite his imagination and curiosity: *Never was there such a town (I thought) for the smell of fish and chips on Saturday nights, for the Saturday afternoon cinema matinees where we shouted and hissed our threepences away; for the crowds in the streets, with leeks in their pockets, on international nights, for the singing that gushed from the smoking doorways of the pubs.*[21] He used to walk the streets late at night savouring the atmosphere of his native town. *I was a lonely night-walker and a steady stander-at-corners, I liked to walk through the wet town ... in dead and empty High Street under the moon, gigantically sad, in the damp streets by ghostly Ebenezer Chapel.*[22]

His letters describe his visits to Gower and the Mumbles. He was particularly attached to the Mermaid and Antelope hotels in this seaside village and called them *these two legendary creatures* that sold *oystered beer*. The wildness of Rhossili also excited his imagination, *Remember the worm, read a meaning into its symbol, a serpent's head, rising out of the clear sea*[23] and he confessed, *I often go down in the mornings to the furthest point of Gower ... the village of Rhossili ... and stay there till evening. The bay is the wildest, bleakest and barreness I know ... four or five miles of yellow coldness going away into the distance of the sea.* [24] *The cliff-perched* seaside village looking down to the sea *white-horsed and full of fishes* was reached by a slow-moving double-decker 'bus and Thomas went either alone or with his friend Raymond Price, *Laughing on the cliff above the very long golden beach, we pointed out to each other, as though the other were blind, the great rock of the Worm's Head. The sea was out. We crossed over on the slipping stones and stood, at last, triumphantly on the windy top. There was monstrous, thick grass there that made us spring-heeled, and we laughed and bounced on it, scaring the sheep who ran up and down the battered sides like goats. Even on the calmest day a wind blew along the Worm ... Why don't we live here always? Always and always. Build a bloody house and live like bloody kings.*[25]

His time on the Swansea newspaper taught him very little about actual writing but it taught him a great deal about growing up. In 1932 at the age of seventeen he was beginning to rebel against provincial life - the small town, the suburban home, nagging relations with all the bickerings and quarrels. Much about family life at 5 Cwmdonkin Drive can be gleaned from the letters of Thomas's elder sister, Nancy. She had met a personable young man, a commercial traveller, named Haydn Taylor and they corresponded regularly. Typical were the comments Nancy wrote on 25. September, 1932. ...*Then last night was Friday night - and that's the day on which Dylan gets paid - he arrived home at 12.15 (midnight). Then there was much row - nowadays, of course, I come in for Pop's nightly nay hourly grumbles ... Thursday night - for the first time in years - Daddy had a night out, arrived home 11.15 and smelt and looked awful ...* (Postscript, Sunday morning.) *When I came to bed last night I wrote four pages to you, telling you of how Dylan arrived home past midnight, very drunk, and of all the horrible things that happened. This morning I tore the letter up ...* [26] Another letter on 7 October, 1932 reads, *This evening Phyllis Bevan and Winnie King arrived. I made coffee for them in the kitchen, Father standing over me saying, This sort of thing must stop, I will not have you making food for half Swansea. If they want to eat tell them to go home.* [27] The rows were invariably about money and drink.

Late in 1932, Thomas lost his job on the *Evening Post* and from then on he was forced to live by his pen and his wits. As Paul Ferris says, *His parents would have been dismayed to realize that apart from one period of three or four years in the 1940s, this state of affairs was to last for the rest of his life.*[28]

The years 1930 - 34 were busy ones for Thomas. His poems began to appear in the small literary magazines and newspapers of London and elsewhere and the young poet began to write his celebrated letters to Pamela Hansford Johnson, his first serious girl friend, Trevor Hughes and others. These letters give an illuminating and detailed picture of his life in Swansea and district and show how much his environment influenced the young poet. We learn from the letters too, about Thomas's reaction to the twentieth century world in which he lived and also his views on politics, religion and sexual experience.

When Thomas was on the *Post*, he met a number of other talented men who were eager to write. First, there was Charles Fisher who became a close friend. Then there was Alfred Janes, an artist whose parents had a greengrocer's shop in Swansea and who came home periodically from his art studies at London. Mervyn Levy, also an artist, was another acquaintance and and so was Wynford Vaughan-Thomas, the famous broadcaster. They met to talk and to drink coffee at the Kardomah café or to drink beer at the Bush Hotel in High Street or in the Mumbles at the Mermaid or Antelope pubs. It was about this time that he met another Swansea friend, someone with strong political views who kept a grocer's shop at 69 Glanbrydan Avenue, opposite Brynmill Park. This was Bert Trick. Trick was interested in literature as well as politics and they played literary games and read poetry together. Trick had enough acumen to realise that Thomas was not so concerned with meaning as with the sounds of the words in his work. In a letter to Bill Read, Birt Trick recalled their first meeting: *I invited him into my sitting room and we sat and discussed all sorts of things, sizing each other up, and after an hour or so, I asked, 'Would you like* (me) *...to read your poems?' And he said, 'Oh, no, poems shouldn't be read; they should be spoken.' Whereupon,* *he pulled a rolled-up blue school exercise book out of his pocket, sat back in the easy chair, with his leg over one arm, and in an arresting voice started to read some of his early poems. I was astonished. It was clear that here was a poet singing in a new voice. After he had read three poems and he had asked me what I thought of them, we discussed them. I was so impressed that I wanted Nell, my wife, to meet him so I went into the next room on grounds of fetching coffee and told Nell, 'I've found a genius. You must come and hear this.' And she, too, immediately fell under the spell of the words and the voice.*[29]

Just before his meetings with Trick, Thomas heard that one of his mother's sisters, Ann Jones, was seriously ill. She ran a farm called *Fern Hill* in north Carmarthenshire where Thomas had spent many happy holidays when he was a young lad. In January, he heard his aunt was dying. She died in 1933: *As I am writing, a telegram arrives. Mother's sister, who is in the Carmarthen Infirmary suffering from cancer of the womb, is dying. There is much lamentation in the family and Mother leaves. This is a well-worn incident in fiction, and one that has happened time after time in real life. The odour of death stinks through a thousand books and a thousand homes. I have rarely encountered it (apart from journalistic enquiries), and find it rather pleasant. It lends a little welcome melodrama to the drawing-room tragi-comedy of my most uneventful life. After Mother's departure I am left alone in the house, feeling slightly theatrical. Telegrams, dying aunts, cancer, especially of such a private part as the womb, distraught mother and unpremeditated train journeys, come rarely. They must be savoured properly and relished in the right spirit. Many summer weeks I spent happily with the cancered aunt on her insanitary farm. She loved me quite inordinately, gave me sweets and money, though she could little afford it, petted, patted and spoiled me. She writes - is it, I wonder, a past tense yet - regularly. Her postscripts are endearing. She still loves - or loved - me, though I don't know why. And now she is dying, or dead, and you will pardon the theatrical writing. Allow me my moment of drama. But the foul thing is I feel utterly unmoved, apart, as I said, from the pleasant death-reek at my negroid nostrils. I haven't really the faintest interest in her or her womb. She is dying. She is dead. She is alive. It is all the same thing. I shall miss her bi-annual postal orders. And yet I like - liked her. She loves - loved me. Am I, he said with the diarist's unctuous, egoistic reactions to his own trivial affairs, callous and hasty? Should I weep? Should I pity the old thing? For a moment I feel I should. There must be something lacking in me. I don't feel worried, or hardly ever, about other people. It's self, self, all the time. I'm rarely interested in other people's emotions, except those of my paste-board characters. I prefer (this is one of the thousand contradictory devils speaking) style to life. My own reactions to emotions rather than the emotions themselves.*[30]

Her death inspired him to write the Ann Jones poem or as it came to be known, *After the Funeral*. Despite his expressed non-caring attitude there is no doubt that Thomas was deeply moved by this tragedy. It is significant that his distress evoked the poem, *And death shall have no dominion*. This was the first poem to be published by a literary magazine for it appeared in *The New English Weekly*. Thomas was only 19 years old.

And death shall have no dominion.
Dead men naked they shall be one
With the man in the wind and the west moon;
When their bones are picked clean and the clean
bones gone,
They shall have stars at elbow and foot;
Though they go mad they shall be sane,
Though they sink through the sea they shall rise
again;
Though lovers be lost love shall not;
And death shall have no dominion.

And death shall have no dominion.
Under the windings of the sea
They lying long shall not die windily;
Twisting on racks when sinews give way,
Strapped to a wheel, yet they shall not break;
Faith in their hands shall snap in two,
And the unicorn evils run them through;
Split all ends up they shan't crack;
And death shall have no dominion.

And death shall have no dominion.
No more may gulls cry at their ears
Or waves break loud on the seashores;
Where blew a flower may a flower no more

Lift its head to the blows of the rain;
Though they be mad and dead as nails,
Heads of the characters hammer through daisies;
Break in the sun till the sun breaks down,
And death shall have no dominion.

Thomas was always interested in words and how they could be used in context; his interest in drama was stimulated by his father at Swansea Grammar School. He took part in a number of plays at school and he joined the Little Theatre, an amateur group that staged plays and revues each year in the Mumbles. In February, 1931, for example, he played Simon Bliss in Noel Coward's *Hay Fever* and later Count Bellair in Farquhar's *Beaux Stratagem* and Witwood in *The Way of The World.* One professional actor commented on his performances saying that *the more fantastic the part ... the better Dylan was.* Some have argued that throughout his life, Thomas was constantly play-acting and that this made him endearing or made him disliked. His time with the theatre group came to an ignominious end when he was preparing to take the male lead in Bernard's *Martine.* The producer, Doreen Goodridge, warned Thomas against going out for a quick drink during rehearsals. She said that if he continued to do this she would replace him. On the night of the dress rehearsal, Thomas could not be found - he had gone out again for a quick bevy. True to her word, the producer dropped him from the play and the event was reported in the local newspaper: *The producer last night had as hard a parcel of luck as anyone can have, the chief male character failed her ... within twenty-four hours ...* [of the first night][31]

It was through the Little Theatre that Thomas met Thomas Taig who produced many of the plays and who later became the first Professor of Drama at Bristol University. Many of Taig's ideas on speech and drama set out in his book, *Rhythm and Metre,* had a great influence on Thomas's dramatic writing, especially on *Under Milk Wood* and how he read his work to audiences.

It was as a young child and as a youth that Thomas grew to love Swansea town. *Never was there such a town,* he wrote and he always believed that. It was the place, the world that made him and he always knew it. His love never changed but remained that of the young child, wrapped around the simple things that are really important.[32] In one of his most famous letters to Pamela Hansford Johnson in October, 1933, he described a typical enjoyable day in Swansea: *At a quarter to ten or thereabouts, breakfast, consisting of an apple, an orange and a banana, is brought to the side of the bed and left there, along with the 'Daily Telegraph' ... the banana is peeled and ... at the last bite, I have read the criminal court cases on page three with great concentration. Downstairs - after another cigarette - I seat myself in front of the fire and commence to read, to read anything that is near, poetry or prose. I read on until twelve or thereabouts ... then down the hill to the Uplands (a lowland collection of crossroads and shops), for one (or perhaps two) pints of beer in the Uplands Hotel. Then home for lunch. After lunch, I retire again to the fire when perhaps I shall read all afternoon ... or merely to write, to write anything, just to let the words and ideas tumble on the sheets of paper, or perhaps I go out, spend the afternoon in walking alone over the very desolate Gower cliffs. After tea I read or write again ... until six o'clock. Then I go to Mumbles - a rather nice village despite its name. I call at the Marine then the Antelope and the Mermaid. If there is a rehearsal, I leave there at 8 o'clock and find my way to the Little Theatre, conveniently situated between the Mermaid and the Antelope. If there is no rehearsal, I continue to commune with these two legendary creatures. Then a three-mile walk home for supper and perhaps more reading, to bed and certainly more writing. Thus drifts an average day. Not a very British day - too much thinkin', too much alcohol.*[33]

That is not to say that he was not critical of Swansea, or critical of elements of Swansea provincialism. He objected to the cosiness of the lower-middle-class world, to the suburban chapel, to the Sunday best - the phrase he used was *snug-suburbed* and by 1934 he wanted to get away from it: *Swansea is a dingy hell, and my mother is a vulgar humbug*[34] he wrote to Pamela Hansford Johnson. He described a visit to Carmarthenshire to her thus: the women are *all breast and bottom*, the colliers *diseased in mind and body as only the Welsh can be ... It's impossible for me to tell you how much I want to get out of it all, out of narrowness and dirtiness, out of the eternal ugliness of the Welsh people, and all that belongs to them, out of the pettiness of a mother I don't care for, and the giggling batch of relatives ...*[35]

But his time in Swansea was the most important period in Dylan's poetic life. As Paul Ferris says, *More than thirty, probably more than forty, of the ninety 'Collected Poems' in their final or near-final versions, as well as others that provided skeletons to go back to later, come from the enclosed world of adolescence that was an end in itself: he never wrote like that again.*[36]

Swansea

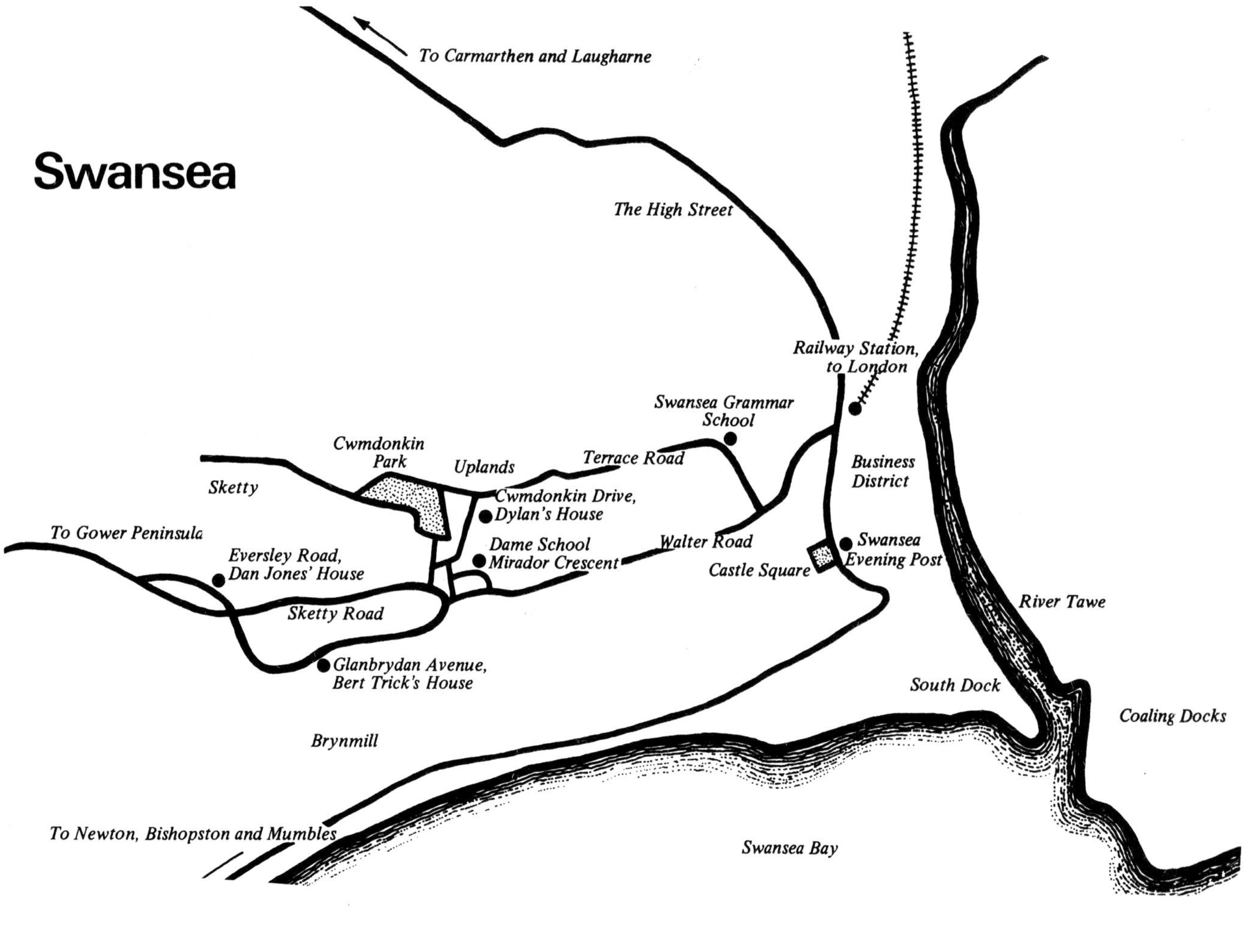

To Carmarthen and Laugharne
The High Street
Railway Station,
to London
Swansea Grammar
School
Cwmdonkin
Park
Uplands
Terrace Road
Business
District
Sketty
Cwmdonkin Drive,
Dylan's House
To Gower Peninsula
Dame School
Mirador Crescent
Walter Road
Swansea
Evening Post
Eversley Road,
Dan Jones' House
Castle Square
Sketty Road
River Tawe
Glanbrydan Avenue,
Bert Trick's House
South Dock
Coaling Docks
Brynmill
To Newton, Bishopston and Mumbles
Swansea Bay

THE SWANSEA DYLAN THOMAS KNEW

The following pages give a brief pictorial representation of the town Thomas knew. They show Swansea as it was from the early twentieth century to the bombing of the town by the Luftwaffe in February, 1941.

Thomas was distraught at the destruction of his beloved town and felt that *our Swansea is dead.*

A later chapter in the book shows photographs of Swansea and West Wales today. Although there have been changes, there are still many places where Thomas would still be at home.

The map opposite shows Swansea in Thomas's time.

THE MUMBLES
Late 1930s

This photograph of The Parade, South End, Mumbles gives a glimpse of what it was like in Thomas's day. Note the empty streets and the single car. It is difficult to move for cars in the Mumbles today.

The Mumbles train (really a tram) ran six miles from Swansea to the Mumbles. A ride in this was a treat to be savoured. On the one side was the glorious sweep of Swansea Bay with its yellow sands and blue sea stretching to meet the sky. On the other was a long narrow road with very little traffic. Thomas often trudged home along this after a night out in the Mumbles. The houses and shops have changed little since his day.

Thomas spent much of his time in the Mumbles then a fishing village, west of Swansea. His maternal Aunt Dosie had married Reverend David Rees who was the minister at Paraclete Church in Newton and young Thomas spent his holidays with them. He loved the place. Later, he became an amateur at the Little Theatre and found friends and companionship in pubs like the Mermaid and Antelope. Sadly, the Mermaid has been destroyed by fire but the Antelope is still there. Apart from the all-pervasive motor car, time has dealt lightly with the village.

MYRDDIN DA
CHEM

OXFORD STREET

This is a photograph of one of the main Swansea shopping areas taken between 1925 - 30. Note the trams which still run on this street and that there are few cars. Most of the women are wearing hats or bonnets, dress which would be considered very formal today. To the right of the picture stood Swansea's main theatre, the Empire. This was famous for variety acts and musicals. Thomas recalled seeing opera there. Later a cinema, the Carlton, was built next door to the Empire. The Empire has been demolished and the Carlton, a listed building, is soon to become a Waterstone's bookshop with the façade preserved. Further down Oxford Street was Swansea Market, still one of the best assets of the town.

In *Old Garbo,* Thomas describes himself passing the time before he meets Mr. Fox. He looks at the theatre queue, inspects the posters and imagines the chorus girls.

SNIPPER BROS LTD
TAILORS
OXFORD STREET, SWANSEA

WIND STREET (1920s)

One of the most popular of Swansea streets in Thomas's day with shops and financial institutions: this photograph shows the most fashionable part of Wind Street (the top end) in the 1920s. (The bottom part was near to the docks and maritime quarter.) On the left at the top of the picture is a glimpse of Ben Evans department store which stood in Castle Bailey Street. It was Swansea's biggest store but was destroyed in the 1941 blitz. At the bottom right hand of the picture is C.A. Sander's, the tobacconist's, a well established Swansea firm which only ceased trading in recent years. No doubt Thomas often went there to buy the Woodbines he was so fond of. This part of town was only about 200 yards from the *South Wales Evening Post* in Castle Street where Thomas worked as a junior reporter.

When Thomas was in Laugharne, he remembered Wind Street with affection. Writing to Charles Fisher in December, 1939, he said that he wished he had *smuts in his eye in Wind Street.*

WAYNES STORES
20
Estelles
20A
Estelles
20A
WAYNES
DELIVERY

SWANSEA TOWN CENTRE

This photograph shows the junction of Dela-Beche Street, Mansel Street and Cradock Street in the 1930s. Travel around the town was by tram and bicycle. On the right is the Albert Hall, which during Thomas's time was a cinema and is now a bingo hall. The house on the opposite corner still stands as do the houses at the top of the photograph. Despite the bombing of the centre of Swansea in 1941, this part of the town escaped almost unscathed although nearby Dynevor School and Swansea Grammar School on Mount Pleasant Hill were not so lucky. Thomas attended the Grammar School from 1925 - 1931 and his father became the Senior English Master. School was a mixed experience for the young Dylan. Delicate but mischievous, he was often the butt of bigger and stronger boys. His unusual ambition to be a poet meant little to his contemporaries. His talent for English and English Literature did not extend to other subjects.

5
SERVICE
COFFEE
DOCKS
YOU
TRIUMPH
STAR
CAFE OPEN TO THE GENERAL PUBLIC

SWANSEA HIGH STREET

In Thomas's day this was the town's main sreet. Note the tram lines and that there are no cars. Thomas spent much of his time in High Street and met his friends regularly at the Café Royal. This was the Kardomah Café, a favourite place where Thomas met Daniel Jones, Alfred Janes, Wynford Vaughan-Thomas and others for coffee and small talk. In *Return Journey,* the Narrator mentions the café and the lost voices o*f poets, painters, and musicians in their beginnings.* The High Street billiards hall was also a favourite as was the Bush Hotel, a pub which still stands today.

High Street features in many of Thomas's stories. The Narrator begins his journey there in *Return Journey* and lists the shops: Eddershaw's, Curry's, Donegal Trading Company, Doctor Scholl's, Burton's, W H Smith, Boots, Leslie's Stores, Upson's Shoes, Prince of Wales Hotel, Tucker's Fish Shop, Stead and Simpson and Hodges the Clothiers. Thomas was also a frequent visitor to the High Street Arcade (now demolished) and Snell's Music Shop there. Just up the road from this picture is Swansea High Street Railway Station, then operated by the Great Western Railway. From there Thomas caught trains to London and elsewhere.

MYRDDIN DA
CHEMI

OXFORD STREET

This is a photograph of one of the main Swansea shopping areas taken between 1925 - 30. Note the trams which still run on this street and that there are few cars. Most of the women are wearing hats or bonnets, dress which would be considered very formal today. To the right of the picture stood Swansea's main theatre, the Empire. This was famous for variety acts and musicals. Thomas recalled seeing opera there. Later a cinema, the Carlton, was built next door to the Empire. The Empire has been demolished and the Carlton, a listed building, is soon to become a Waterstone's bookshop with the façade preserved. Further down Oxford Street was Swansea Market, still one of the best assets of the town.

In *Old Garbo*, Thomas describes himself passing the time before he meets Mr. Fox. He looks at the theatre queue, inspects the posters and imagines the chorus girls.

SNIPPER BROS LTD
TAILORS
OXFORD STREET, SWANSEA

WIND STREET (1920s)

One of the most popular of Swansea streets in Thomas's day with shops and financial institutions: this photograph shows the most fashionable part of Wind Street (the top end) in the 1920s. (The bottom part was near to the docks and maritime quarter.) On the left at the top of the picture is a glimpse of Ben Evans department store which stood in Castle Bailey Street. It was Swansea's biggest store but was destroyed in the 1941 blitz. At the bottom right hand of the picture is C.A. Sander's, the tobacconist's, a well established Swansea firm which only ceased trading in recent years. No doubt Thomas often went there to buy the Woodbines he was so fond of. This part of town was only about 200 yards from the *South Wales Evening Post* in Castle Street where Thomas worked as a junior reporter.

When Thomas was in Laugharne, he remembered Wind Street with affection. Writing to Charles Fisher in December, 1939, he said that he wished he had *smuts in his eye in Wind Street.*

WIND STREET, SWANSEA.

WIND STREET, 1935

This is a later photograph of Wind Street probably taken in 1935 but there are still trams. Horses and carts are still being used extensively but there is more evidence of cars. This area was well known to Thomas when he worked on the *Post* and he was a frequent visitor to the Metropole Hotel on the left of the picture. In *Return Journey*, Thomas as a young journalist attended an auction there. The hotel has now been demolished.

METROPOLE
DANN & Co
Hatters & Hosiers
Outfitters
CLOTHIERS

SOUTH WALES EVENING POST
CASTLE STREET

These were the offices of the *South Wales Evening Post* where Thomas worked as a junior reporter from 1931 to 1932 (although the photograph was actually taken some time after Thomas had left the *Post*). Immediately behind these offices is the Old Swansea Castle. The *Post* has now moved to new premises at the bottom of Wind Street.

Thomas wrote articles and material for both the *South Wales Evening Post* and the *Herald of Wales.* It is perhaps, understandable that he was not very good as a reporter. He preferred the world of the imagination to the cold world of facts and he soon lost his job.

EVENING POST · HERALD OF WALES

CASTLE STREET, 1938

This later shot of Castle Street shows the changes that came about just before the 1939 - 45 World War. Horses, carts and trams have disappeared, replaced by buses and cars. This Street was important for the poet's parents because they were married in Castle Street Congregational Church on 30 December, 1903.

This was the town Thomas knew well but within three years it was all to change, devastated by the blitz of 1941, and the Swansea Dylan loved, to use his own words, *was dead.*

KARDOMAH
CAFE

THE BBC STUDIO AT THE GROVE, UPLANDS

This well-known photograph dated 24 October, 1949 shows Thomas at the BBC in their Grove Studio in the Uplands. It is interesting from a number of points of view. First, it shows the poet with some of his best friends. Vernon Watkins is sitting far left opposite Thomas and Daniel Jones is next to him. The picture also includes John Pritchard, Alfred Janes who painted several portraits of Thomas and John Griffiths. Secondly, the Studio was situated in the Grove just down the road from the house in Cwmdonkin Drive where Thomas was born. Visiting the Grove must have been a nostalgic experience for Thomas with memories of Ferguson's sweetshop and the 'flea pit' cinema. Also at the back of the Grove is the lower entrance to Cwmdonkin Park where he spent many happy hours as a child.

THE OLD GUILDHALL

This very early photograph (Victorian, post 1857) is included as a contrast to the picture later in the book of the centre today. This 'Old Guildhall' has been tastefully refurbished and virtually rebuilt and re-opened as the Dylan Thomas Centre.

Southwest Wales

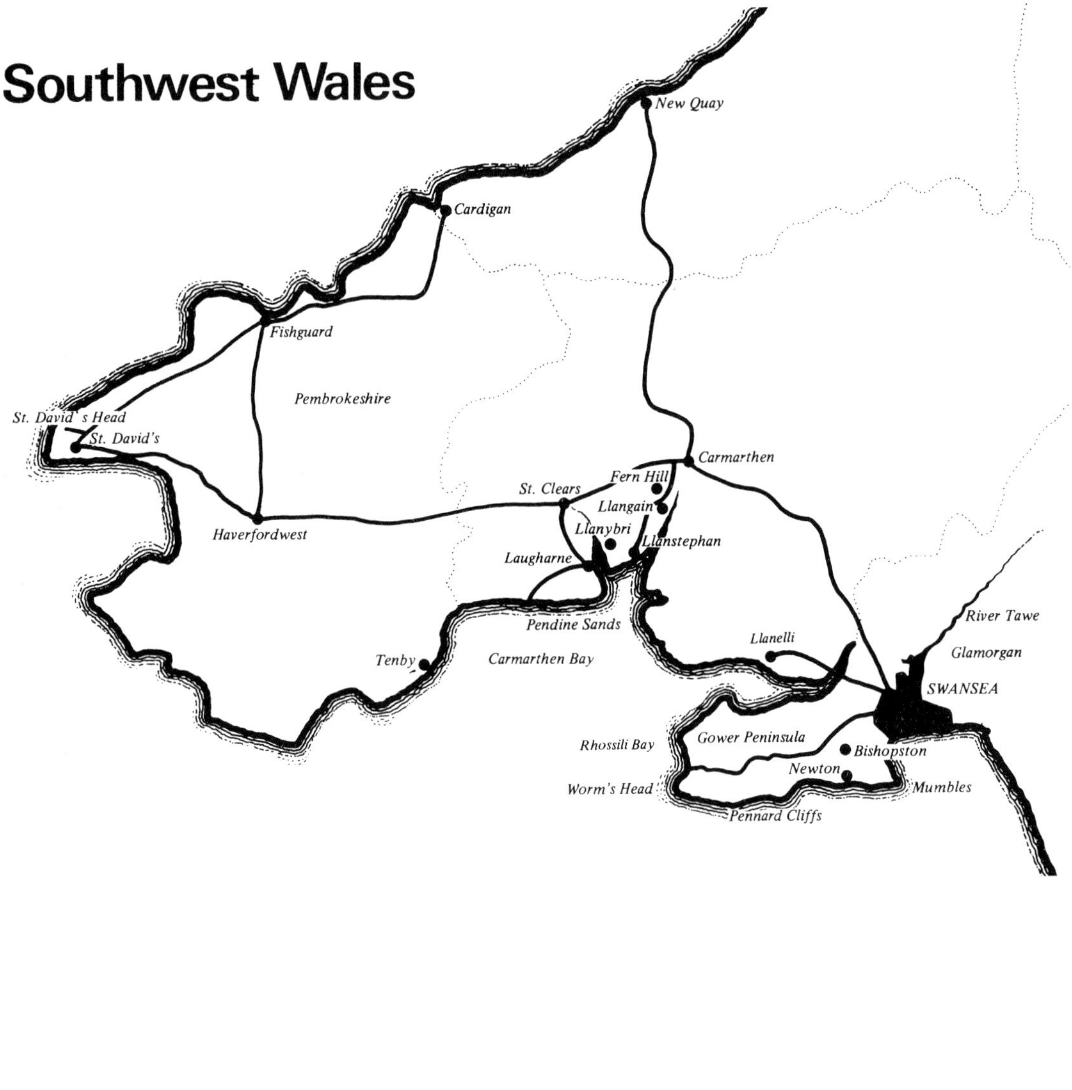

EXILE AND RETURN, 1934 - 1949

The land of my fathers. My fathers can keep it. These were the reported words of Thomas when he left for London in November, 1934. But he did not mean it. He kept popping back to Swansea and West Wales to see his parents, other relations and to continue writing. It was only in Wales that he could work. He needed the familiar surroundings where he had been so happy as a young boy. *In London where he had so many social contacts and where so many dramatic tasks were expected of him, he could not work at all.* [37] But he did not return permanently to his homeland until 1949.

Thomas himself recalls that from time to time he was terribly *nostalgic* ... about *the town of Swansea* and his exile was not at all to his liking, *in London, where we were exiled bohemian boily boys ... three very young monsters green and brimming from Swansea ... all living together in one big boring beautiful room ... in Redcliffe Gardens ... that's when the portrait of me, a frog in his salad days was painted.* His imaginative vitality never left Wales or Swansea: he returned constantly to live and to write in his native land whether he came from London, Hampshire or Oxford. He usually stayed in Laugharne or at his parents' house in Bishopston, near Swansea. He also spent a year during this period at New Quay, West Wales. He had a particular liking for Laugharne and he high-lighted this in his broadcast on the town ('Quite Early One Morning'), *And some, like myself, just came, one day for the day, and never left; got off the bus, and forgot to get on again. Whatever the reason, if any, for our being here, in this timeless, mild, beguiling island of a town with its seven public houses, one chapel in action, one church, one factory, two billiard tables, one St. Bernard (without brandy), one policeman, three rivers, a visiting sea, one Rolls Royce selling fish and chips, one cannon (cast-iron), one chancellor (flesh and blood) ... and a multitude of fixed birds ...*

By this time, Thomas had had a number of love affairs. His first serious affair was with Pamela Hansford Johnson (later a novelist and the wife of Lord (C P) Snow). She lived with her mother in Battersea and wrote to Thomas about his poem *That sanity be kept* saying how much she liked it. They did not meet until February, 1934 but corresponded regularly.

Unfortunately, all her letters have disappeared but twenty-five of those written by Thomas have survived. In them he talks about life and family and describes the problems of his father who had been diagnosed as having cancer of the mouth.

Their love affair was tempestuous but brief and by early 1935 it was over. In March, Thomas was ill and came to Swansea to recuperate. It did not take long. There was a warm welcome at Bert Trick's shop, Thomas's father had recovered and was back teaching and his old friends still met at the Kardomah. Swansea and Wales had come to his rescue once again.

In the spring of 1935 on one of his many visits to Swansea, Thomas met a young man who was to be one of his closest friends. This was Vernon Watkins. Watkins had bought a copy of Thomas's *18 Poems* (which had been published on 18th. December, 1934) and then bumped into David Rees, the retired minister from the Mumbles who was married to Thomas's Aunt Dosie. Watkins asked for the poet's address and wrote to him. Soon after this they met on the cliffs at Pennard where Watkins lived. They got on well and respected each other as poets and critics. Watkins supported Thomas throughout his life and even when he let him down at his wedding (Thomas was best man and did not turn up) Watkins forgave him.

It was at this time (March, 1935) that Thomas accepted an invitation to stay at a cottage in Derbyshire. His hosts were a young historian, A J P Taylor (soon to make a name for himself as a brilliant historical analyst) and his young Welsh-born wife, Margaret, who was something of a dilettante and interested in the Arts. She became one of Thomas's staunchest supporters and benefactors and as she had money of her own she contributed to the poet's living expenses for the rest of his life. She also provided accommodation for him in various homes throughout his writing career.

Almost a year later, Thomas met the love of his life, Caitlin Macnamara. She was very beautiful with bright blue eyes and a thick mass of curly blonde hair. For a time she worked as a chorus girl at the London Palladium and then danced elsewhere. Eventually, she came under the influence of Augustus John, the artist, and she often sat for him. By 19th. October, 1936 it was clear that Thomas has fallen in love with her and on 11th. July, 1937 they were married in Penzance Registry Office. At first they lived with her mother in Blashford, Ringwood, Hampshire but ten months later (May, 1938) they moved to their first proper home in Laugharne, West Wales. This was a cottage in Gosport Street but in late July they moved to *Sea View*, a large detatched residence *at the posh end of the town.*

By this time, Thomas was virtually penniless. The family begged or borrowed furniture, Caitlin made stews or boiled fresh cockles. They used candles instead of electricity (at this time electricity had not reached *Sea View*). Vernon Watkins said later that this time at *Sea View* was one of the happiest in Thomas's life. In a letter to Bert Trick on 29th. September, Thomas told of his financial difficulties and about how he was writing *Portrait of the Artist as a Young Dog* which he described succinctly as *stories towards a provincial biography ... They are all about Swansea life; the pubs, clubs, billiard rooms, promenades, adolescence and suburban nights, friendships, tempers and humiliations.* Occasionally, he visited Vernon Watkins's house in Pennard, Gower to discuss poetry.

His shortage of money at this time was chronic and he borrowed from anyone who would lend. Thomas returned to London again to try to raise funds. One of the main reasons for leaving Wales at this time was to escape debtors and it is clear that neither Caitlin nor Dylan wanted to stay away. To add to their difficulties, Caitlin was now pregnant with their first child and went home to her mother to have the baby. A son, Llewelyn Edouard Thomas, was born on 30 January, 1939 and Thomas was now determined to improve his financial position. He wrote to Bert Trick about the new baby and the letter was full of nostalgia for Swansea and West Wales. They still owed £30 in Laugharne and were not able to pay it until May, 1939 when they returned to *Sea View.*

Because they were short of money, the family was forced to move back to London again and lived in Chelsea from 1942 to 1944. There his daughter, Aeronwy, was born in March, 1943. He was still unhappy away from Wales and by 1944 had resolved to return again to the Principality. On 30 August, 1944, he wrote to Vernon Watkins saying that he was to live in New Quay. A few months later, Thomas settled in his new home *made of wood and asbestos* and situated *in a really wonderful bit of the bay.*

It was here that he wrote *Quite Early One Morning* which he read on the B.B.C. Welsh Home Service. It describes the poet's walk through a small Welsh town near the sea and gives an account of the inhabitants, their aspirations and dreams. It is clearly the birth of the idea which culminated some years later in *Under Milk Wood.*

Because of his poor health, especially trouble with his chest and asthma, Thomas was ineligible for military service in the War and he did a great deal of work for the B.B.C. and worked on film scripts at this time.

Swansea suffered three nights of terror when the Luftwaffe razed the centre of the town to the ground. Thomas wrote a script entitled *Return Journey* for the B.B.C. which was first broadcast on the Home Service on 15th. June, 1947. He described a walk through the devastated Swansea looking for someone after fourteen years.

Narrator: What's the Three Lamps like now?
Customer: It isn't like anything. It isn't there. It's nothing mun. You remember Ben Evans's stores? It's right next door to that. Ben Evans isn't there either.

Despite the devastation, the heart of Swansea still lived. In Thomas's view nothing could really change it: *the ugly, lovely at least to me, town is alive, exciting and real though war has made a hideous hole in it. I do not need to remember a dream. The reality is there. The fine, live people, the spirit of Wales itself.*[38]

By this time Thomas's poetry was reaching maturity. He began to produce what is regarded as his best work, the poetry and prose of joyous recollection. He re-created his childhood experiences in *Fern Hill* and his work became visionary and mystical. For him, childhood, with its intimations of immortality, was a state of innocence and grace. The fact that Thomas had suffered the loss of his aunt heightened the pathos and deepened his vision of his childhood days. *Fern Hill* is Thomas at his best. He evokes the joys, mysteries and wonders of childhood through a series of images and plays on words that appeal to all the senses.

FERN HILL

Now as I was young and easy under the apple boughs
About the lilting house and happy as the grass was green,
The night above the dingle starry,
Time let me hail and climb
Golden in the heydays of his eyes,
And honoured among wagons I was prince of the apple towns
And once below a time I lordly had the trees and leaves
Trail with daisies and barley
Down the rivers of the windfall light.

And as I was green and carefree, famous among the barns
About the happy yard and singing as the farm was home,
In the sun that is young once only,
Time let me play and be
Golden in the mercy of his means,
And green and golden I was huntsman and herdsman, the calves
Sang to my horn, the foxes on the hills barked clear and cold,
And the sabbath rang slowly

In the pebbles on the holy streams.

All the sun long it was running, it was lovely, the hay
Fields high as the house, the tunes from the chimneys, it was air
And playing, lovely and watery
And fire green as grass.
And nightly under the simple stars
As I rode to sleep the owls were bearing the farm away,
All the moon long I heard, blessed among stables, the nightjars
Flying with the ricks, and the horses
Flashing into the dark.

And then to awake, and the farm like a wanderer white
With the dew, come back, the cock on his shoulder: it was all
Shining, it was Adam and maiden,
The sky gathered again
And the sun grew round that very day.
So it must have been after the birth of the simple light
In the first, spinning place, the spellbound horses walking warm
Out of the whinnying green stable
On to the fields of praise.

And honoured among foxes and pheasants by the gay house
Under the new made clouds and happy as the heart was long.
In the sun born over and over,
I ran my heedless ways,
My wishes raced through the house high hay
And nothing I cared, at my sky blue trades, that time allows

In all his tuneful turning so few and such morning songs
Before the children green and golden
Follow him out of grace.

Nothing I care, in the lamb white days, that time would take me
Up to the swallow thronged loft by the shadow of my hand.
In the moon that is always rising,
Nor that riding to sleep
I should hear him fly with the high fields
And wake to the farm forever fled from the childless land.
Oh as I was young and easy in the mercy of his means,
Time held me green and dying
Though I sang in my chains like the sea.

This is probably his most famous poem and it is typically nostalgic about the time when he was at the home of his maternal aunt enjoying life as a young boy.

Life was good for Thomas at the end of the Second World War. In the three years which began in October, 1945, he worked fairly regularly for the B.B.C. The late John Arlott admired him greatly, *I worked with him some twenty or thirty times a year from 1945 to 1950, on literary programmes of every type. He was always open-minded to experiment ... and his very real integrity made him the prefect touchstone for a producer.*[39] Louis MacNeice was also an admirer: *He was ... a subtle and versatile actor, as he proved repeatedly in radio performances. And he 'took production'. Though his special leaning (as was natural, given his astonishing voice) was to the sonorous and emotional, he enjoyed playing character parts, especially comic or grotesque ones, such as a friendly Raven which he played for me once in a dramatised Norwegian folk-tale. He could even 'throw away' if required to. And in all these sidelines - as in all his verse and prose - there appeared the same characteristc blend of delight in what he was doing and care as to how he did it.*[40]

Thomas was so relaxed that the whole family went on holiday to Dublin and Kerry: *We ate ourselves daft: lobsters, steaks, cream, hills of butter, homemade bread, chicken and chocolates: we drank Seithenyns of porter and Guinness: we walked, climbed, rode on donkeys, bathed, sailed, rowed, danced, sang.*[41]

By the end of the Second World War (1945), Thomas had conceived the idea of a visit to America. The following year, his volume of *Selected Writings* was published in America. This meant that his work became very popular in the States. He had an American benefactor in John Malcolm Brinnin and an American publisher in New Directions. Five years were to elapse before he could go, however, and in this interim period he and his growing family had to eat and live. In September, 1945 he had a short stay in St. Stephen's Hospital, London and was diagnosed as having 'alcoholic gastritis.' After this time, the family went to live in the summerhouse provided by Thomas's staunchest patron, Margaret Taylor, at their home *Holywell Ford*, Oxford. For the rest of his life, the poet and his family lived either rent free or paid the minimum for accommodation provided by Mrs. Taylor.

By now, Thomas should have been fairly well off because he was receiving money from his book, *Deaths and Entrances*, published by Dent in February, 1946. They also published *Twenty-Five Poems*, *Map of Love* and *Portrait of the Artist* which all started to sell quite well. Also, in New York, New Directions was promoting and selling his writings and he was working very regularly for the B.B.C. on radio. He was also invited to give occasional readings and took part in discussions which brought in further income. But money did not last in Thomas's hands. Much of it went on entertainment, travelling and drink and the Inland Revenue began pursuing him in 1947 - 48.

In April, 1947 the whole family went to Italy where Thomas hoped to improve his health and spend some time writing but the trip was not a success. He was also tired of living in the Taylor's summerhouse and he wrote to Margaret Taylor asking her to find suitable alternative accommodation for his family when they returned to the UK: *I do hope that you can help us to find a house in or near Oxford, so that we see each other again ... I want, so much, to come back to Oxford. Oh, anywhere a house. I am lost without one. I am domestic as a slipper. I want somewhere of my own. I'm old enough now. I want a house to shout, sleep and work in. Please help; though I deserve nothing.*[42] After this plea, Margaret Taylor scoured the Oxford countryside and eventually found them a home in the village of South Leigh. She renovated it and offered it to Thomas and his family at a peppercorn rent of a pound a week. For most of the time that he lived in South Leigh, Thomas was thinking about Wales. He reasoned that if Margaret Taylor could afford to buy them a house in Oxfordshire, she might be persuaded to buy them a home in Swansea or West Wales. He longed to return to Laugharne. To one of his friends he wrote that if he could live there he could work half the year on film scripts and the other half on his own poems and stories. He wrote to another friend who worked for the magazine *Picture Post* offering an article on the place: *I really do know it* (Laugharne) *intimately, love it beyond all places in Wales, and have longed for years to write something about it (a radio play I am writing has Laugharne, though not by name, as its setting).*[43]

He wrote to Margaret Taylor about a possible move to Laugharne and when they met he again begged most persuasively. She responded magnificently and negotiated several times for houses in Laugharne throughout 1948 but the deals fell through. Fortunately, in the spring of 1949 the *Boat House* came up for sale. Margaret Taylor moved swiftly to clinch the sale paying £10,500 for it. In May, Thomas and his family moved there and agreed to pay a modest rent to their benefactor. His parents moved into a cottage called *The Pelican* near Brown's Hotel. Thomas's satisfaction was expressed by his friend in the introduction to the *Letters of Vernon Watkins: The peace and beauty of this small sea-town beyond Carmarthen, a fishing village at the end of the world, represented for him the last refuge of life and sanity in a nightmare world.*[44]

LAUGHARNE

During his short life, Dylan Thomas moved around a great deal living in many places and visiting others. These included Swansea, Cornwall, Hampshire, London, Ireland, France, Italy, Iran, Elba, Oxford, South Leigh (Oxfordshire) and the United States of America. But wherever he lived he always came back to Swansea and Laugharne, especially Laugharne: he moved to and from this small Carmarthenshire town all his life.

Laugharne is in reality a small fishing village with pretensions of grandeur. It has changed little since Thomas lived there. It was granted a Royal Charter in 1307 which still controls the government of the town. There is a corporation consisting of a Portreeve, two Common Attorneys, one Recorder, four Constables, a Bailiff or Crier and a Foreman of the Jury. The Grand Jury of twenty men under a Foreman meets in the Town Hall every fourteen days: the Chairman is the Portreeve. The old Town Hall dates from 1745 and Thomas would have seen it as he passed up Wogan Street.

Thomas had a great affection for the place and he explained in one of his letters how he knew it intimately and how he loved it beyond all other places in Wales. Largely through the generosity of Margaret Taylor he returned there in the spring of 1949 and lived in the *Boat House* which stood under a sea-cliff a little away from the town.

The *Boat House* and its setting may seem romantic. It is isolated, lonely with only the estuary and birds for company, but it was not the ideal place in which to live, especially for Thomas who from childhood suffered with his chest. The coast shielded the house from the worst of the south westerlies but during the winter, there were constant drizzles and sea mists. The house itself was damp and had been left to fall into a poor state of repair. The woodwork was spongy and damp stained the ceilings, a verandah or balcony which was on two sides of the house was weak and had been strengthened by tin squares. When the family took up residence there was no piped water and until they were connected to the mains they had to carry water from a well outside. Rats were a constant problem and often scuttled into the house or could be heard scampering below the house and in the roof space. In the lane above the house called Cliff Walk was a bicycle shed which belonged to the

LAUGHARNE
and surrounding area

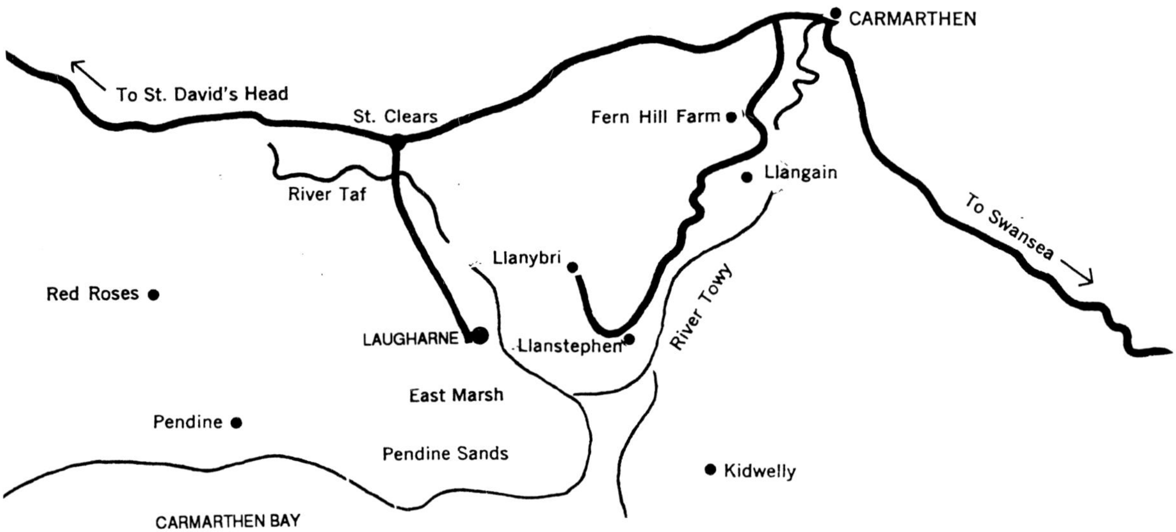

premises. This was reached by steep steps coming up from the *Boat House* below.

Despite the rather delapidated state of the house, the location was magnificent for it overlooked the estuary below where three rivers converge into tidal flats and sandbanks. The *Boat House* was away from the noise of traffic and all that could be heard was the sound of water-birds, seagulls and at night the hooting of a solitary owl. This was what Thomas liked about the place - its quietness and solitude - and as long as he could leave it occasionally to visit nearby Carmarthen or the hustle and bustle of his native Swansea he was content.

Thomas was idealistic about the village and told how he *Came one day for the day, and never left, got off the bus and forgot to get on again*. The bicycle shed became his workroom and from its window he had a bird's eye view of the estuary, including Sir John's Hill which is the subject of one of his poems. In the other direction he could see the *Boat House* and the gardens and green fields stretching away from the township. It is no wonder that his poems are so full of the imagery of water-birds, seagulls and birds of prey. Laugharne is a quiet, solitary place (especially off-peak and out of season) and here Thomas could work peacefully and pay frequent visits to Brown's Hotel only a stone's throw away. He called the *Boat House* his *sun shaken house on a breakneck of rocks* ... and it is probably Laugharne Castle that he recalled with his description of a *castle brown as owls.*

In his lifetime Thomas never owned the *Boat House* but he was ever thankful to his most consistent benefactor, Margaret Taylor, for buying it for him and his family and renting it to them.

It is difficiult to assess how much writing Thomas actually did in Laugharne during the four and a half years before he died in November, 1953. Paul Ferris says that he wrote only six complete poems in that time and John Brinnin, his American agent, was critical of the unfinished work he found there after Thomas's death.

The poems *When I Work, Poem in October, Over Sir John's Hill, Poem on His Birthday* and the *Prologue* have settings which are easily recognisable as Laugharne and the prose, *Under Milk Wood,* his most famous work, is Laugharne, warts and all. His recurring image for Laugharne is hardly complimentary. He described it as a *dead* place: he called it *this idyllic tomb* but even on his first visit he was attracted to it: *the strangest town in Wales ... Today ... a hell-mouthed mist is blowing over the Laugharne ferry.* He told Henry Treece, the poet, that the town had *three good pubs and ... the best bottled mild.* Writing an invitation to Bert Trick, his Swansea friend, he called the place *this cockled city ... sweet and quiet ... so slow and prettily sad.* But it was not all happiness there. To Charles Fisher he wrote *the castle and the pretty water make me sick* and to an American friend living in Italy he wrote the *weather gets me like poverty: it blows and then blinds, creeps chalky and crippling into the bones, shrouds me in wet self, rains away the world.* In 1953, he wrote to Brinnin that to him, Laugharne meant *turpor and rain and Joy's dungeon.* (Joy was the innkeeper at Brown's Hotel where Thomas used to drink.)

As one would expect Thomas's writing is full of the images of Laugharne. To name only a few in *Quite Early One Morning*, Laugharne is *this timeless, beautiful, barmy town ... a legendary lazy little black-magical bedlam by the sea.* It is *the dwindling harbour* of *Poem in October* and the *Crystal harbour vale,Where the sea cobbles sail* , of *Over Sir John's Hill.*

DYLAN THOMAS, POETRY AND PROSE

Dylan Thomas heralded a new kind of poetry in the 20th. century. It was so different from the realism of Eliot and Auden and the social commentaries written by other 20th. century writers. Thomas was a romantic whose work was devoid of social issues: he did not feel the need for reforming the world but took it at its face value. In an age of impersonality, Thomas was essentially personal and he used his work to examine the major issues that concerned him. He sang from the depths of his being about life, death, sin, redemption, the natural processes, sex, creation and decay.

'Sang' has been used deliberately because the first quality that strikes the reader of his poetry is its lyrical, musical quality.[45] This is even clearer listening to the poet reading his own work. Thomas's early writing was strongly criticized as being obscure. People argued that it was sound only, gibberish, with no meaning or sense to it. Today, this poetry is recognized for what it is: the perfect fusion of sound and sense derived from a careful selection of words, phrases, images, rhythm and rhyme. David Daiches remarks in 'The Poetry of Dylan Thomas' *for all the appearance of spontaneity and sometimes of free association that his poems present to readers, Thomas was a remarkably conscientious craftsman for whom meaning was bound with pattern and order. No modern poet in English has had a keener sense of form or has handled stanzas and verse paragraphs - whether traditional or original - with more deliberate cunning.*[46]

Thomas realised the problem for his readers. He said that his poetry was rigorously compressed. It was to this quality that he referred when he said that his words contained *no diffusion or dilution* and that everything was tightly packed as in a *mad-doctor's bag*. He reached a point where his language implied so much that it seemed to say very little and he was aware of this in April,1936 when he was finishing his sonnets. Consider these lines:

> *If my head hurt a hair's foot*
> *Pack back the downed bone. If the unpricked ball of my breath*
> *Bump on a spout let the bubbles jump out.*

Sooner drop with the worm of the ropes round my throat
Than bully ill love to the clouted scene.[47]

Thomas's early works were criticized in other respects. Critics argued that they were concerned solely with birth, death and copulation. However, in his consideration of these subjects, Thomas was working out the main themes of all his poetic work, the unity of life and death, birth and decay, and the cyclical nature of life itself.

An understanding of Thomas's poetry comes from examining the verse and from explanations in his letters. Thus, when only 19, in a letter to Pamela Hansford Johnson he gave an account of the role of the 'physical' in his work (relating this to comments by John Donne) and stressing the importance of the 'body' in his concept of poetry. Later in 1945, in a letter to Vernon Watkins, he showed how critical he was of his own work and made a judgement on his own development: *I'm so glad you wrote the last bit about the poems: how you so much more liked the latest to the earliest. Wouldn't it be hell if it was the other way around, and the words were coming quicker and slicker and weaker and wordier every day and, by comparison, one's first poems in adolescence seemed, to one, like flying-fish islands never to be born in again? Thank god, writing is daily more difficult ... and that the result, if only to you and me, is worth all the discarded shocks, the reluctantly shelved grand moony images, cut-and-come again cardpack references.* It is evident from this that Thomas took infinite care with his work, he was a perfectionist par excéllence. The time and patience he took was emphasized by a letter written to F. F. Bozman in 1952. In this he explained why he wrote a verse *Prologue* for the forthcoming *Collected Poems* and the difficult technical task he set himself in the structure of his poetry. Thomas worked on this *Prologue* for two whole months and would not sacrifice this preface for one which he could complete more easily. He said: *I am a painstaking, conscientious, involved and devious craftsman in words, however unsuccessful the result so often appears, and to whatever wrong uses I may apply my technical paraphernalia.* In his *Poetic Manifesto*, he wrote *I use everything and anything to make my poems work and move in the direction I want them to: old tricks, new tricks, puns, portmanteau - words, paradox, allusion, paranomasia, paragram, catachresis, slang assonantal ryhmes, vowel rhymes, sprung rhythm. Every device there is in language is there to be used if you will. Poets have ... to enjoy themselves sometimes, and the twistings and convolutions ... are all part of the joy.*[48]

To Charles Fisher, he wrote: *I like things that are difficult to write and difficult to understand ... I like contradicting my images, saying two things at once in one word, four in two and one in six.*

Thomas's poetry has an overall sensory appeal. He uses poetic features such as imagination, imagery, symbolism, word plays, analogy, detail, atmosphere, colour and rhyme in combination. All these features produce a poetry with superb texture which has not been surpassed. Because of the sensuous quality, the care for detail and the use of language and rhythm, Thomas's poetry is an exciting experience for the reader and even more so for the listener:

Altarwise by owl-light in the half-way house
The gentleman lay graveward with his furies;
Abaddon in the hangnail cracked from Adam,
And, from his fork, a dog among the fairies,
The atlas-eater with a jaw for news,
Bit out the mandrake with tomorrow's scream.[49]

Thomas's work can be compared to the poetry of three other writers, Eliot, Keats and Donne. Like much of Eliot's work, Thomas's poetry is a real challenge to the reader. He does not develop the poems through logic but through imagery, verbal play, repetition and other devices of style. Thomas realised the importance of metaphor and simile in his work.Writing to Henry Treece he said, *A poem by myself needs a host of images, because its centre is a host of images.* Notice, for example, image following image in this first stanza from *Especially When the October Wind.*

Especially when the October wind
With frosty fingers punishes my hair,
Caught by the crabbing sun I walk on fire
And cast a shadow crab upon the land,
By the sea's side, hearing the noise of birds,
Hearing the raven cough in winter sticks,
My busy heart who shudders as she talks
Sheds the syllabic blood and drains her words.

To consider only a few images, note the personification of the October wind with her *frosty fingers* and the dual metaphors of the *crabbing sand* and *walking on fire* re-emphasized by the *crab-like shadow* in the next line. Note too the deliberate use of the words *cough* and *sticks* in the next line, the first so reminiscent of humans and the second declaring the bareness of winter as it descends upon the countryside: the poet forecasts the death and destruction of the coming winter.

The imagery is reminiscent of the work of Keats, who like Thomas, insisted on the importance of sound and rhythm. Thomas also has an affinity with Donne. *Deaths and Entrances* confirms Thomas is a religious poet or a poet with an intimate knowledge of the Christian ethic. (Vernon Watkins always insisted that he was a religious poet in the broadest sense.) Thomas owed his biblical echoes and imagery, his religious tensions, his Puritan conflicts to his Welsh upbringing and background. There is extensive use of Christian myth and symbol in his work, and there is a note of formal ritual and incantation emphasizing that in many senses Thomas is a preacher in verse. It must be admitted, of course, that Thomas denies and defies the practices and beliefs of Christianity: that he rejects organised religion; that his attitude to the Holy Eucharist is sacrilegious (*This Bread I Break*) but nevertheless his personal mythology relies extensively on biblical and religious symbols.[50]

Professor Moynihan writing on *The Craft and Art of Dylan Thomas* refers to three periods in the poet's work. These are the first period from 1925 - 1935 when he wrote straightforward, easily understood verse; the second period from 1936 - 1938 when Thomas's poetry was obscure and then from 1939 to 1953 when his poetry grew slowly clearer until it was extremely lucid in *Under MIlk Wood*. In the same way Professor Moynihan shows that the early work of Thomas is principally concerned with themes of revolt, the middle work with themes and situations of reflection and debate and the late work with themes of praise and consent.[51]

Let us now briefly discuss Thomas's poetic techniques in respect of two of his best known poems.

AFTER THE FUNERAL

(In memory of Ann Jones)

After the funeral, mule praises, brays,
Windshake of sailshaped ears, muffle-toed tap
Tap happily on one peg in the thick
Grave's foot, blinds down the lids, the teeth in black,
The spittled eyes, the salt ponds in the sleeves,
Morning smack of the spade that wakes up sleep,

Shakes a desolate boy who slits his throat
In the dark of the coffin and sheds dry leaves,
That breaks one bone to light with a judgement clout,
After the feast of tear-stuffed time and thistles
In a room with a stuffed fox and a stale fern,
I stand, for this memorial's sake, alone
In the snivelling hours with dead, humped Ann
Whose hooded, fountain heart once fell in puddles
Round the parched worlds of Wales and drowned each sun
(Though this for her is a monstrous image blindly
Magnified out of praise; her death was a still drop;
She would not have me sinking in the holy
Floor of her heart's fame; she would lie dumb and deep
And need no druid of her broken body).
But I, Ann's bard on a raised hearth; call all
The seas to service that her wood-tongued virtue
Babble like a bellbuoy over the hymning heads,
Bow down the walls of the ferned and foxy woods
That her love sing and swing through a brown chapel,
Bless her bent spirit with four, crossing birds.
Her flesh was meek as milk, but this skyward statue
With the wild breast and blessed and giant skull
Is carved from her in a room with a wet window
In a fiercely mourning house in a crooked year.
I know her scrubbed and sour humble hands
Lie with religion in their cramp, her threadbare
Whisper in a damp word, her wits drilled hollow,
Her fist of a face died clenched on a round pain;

And sculptured Ann is seventy years of stone.
These cloud-sopped, marble hands, this monumental
Argument of the hewn voice, gesture and psalm
Storm me forever over her grave until
The stuffed lung of the fox twitch and cry Love
And the strutting fern lay seeds on the black sill.[52]

In this poem, Thomas begins by describing the mules pulling the hearse, the sealing of the coffin, the hypocritical grief of the mourners, and the noise of the spade shovelling the earth (lines 1 - 6). He is grief-stricken and wishes to record this grief and illustrates the reasons for it. But his grief is not as intense as he would have wished (lines 7 - 15) and he wants to make his love for the dead woman immortal. He makes an exaggerated eulogy of his maternal aunt which contrasts with her simplicity (lines 16 - 30) and with the finality of her death (lines 31 - 40). Professor Moynihan has shown that besides the argument and images already discussed the whole poem is overlaid with another central imagae. He calls this a *central seed* which is, in reality, an expanded metaphor. This is, water is life, dryness is death. *Nearly everything in the poem depends on the central water metaphor, and nearly everything pertains to dryness and water, always with the life-death, fertile-infertile associations natural to the terms throughout.*[53]

In *Fern Hill* (see pages 56 - 58) we have an example of Thomas's poetry at its best. Here he evokes the joys, mysteries and wonders of childhood. There are rhythmic variations, numerous short prepositions *(over, under* and *about),* colour words and phrases, *green* and *golden, golden in the mercy of his means* and *wanderer white,* assonance and alliteration. Another feature is the inversion and consequent revitalizing of worn out phrases - *all the sun long* instead of *all the day long. Once below a time* instead of *Once upon a time* and *All the moon long* instead of *All night.* (The refurbished cliché is one of Thomas's most important artifices). Besides, there are carefully contrived repetitions and the rhythmic alternation of long and short lines and strong and weak stresses. The change to *Adam and maiden* instead of *Adam and Eve* is particularly significant with the connotation of innocence and purity that the first phrase brings. Structurally, the pattern of the stanzas emphasizes Thomas's concern for symmetry in his work. The rhythm is based on stress rather than metre: short lines have three stresses and the long ones six. The effect of line length, alternating rhythm and strong and weak stresses produces a breathlessness coming from the awe and wonder of childhood experience. The slowing down at the end of most of the stanzas is reinforced by the rolling last line: *Though I sang in my chains like the sea.*

We cannot leave these brief notes about Thomas's poetry without saying a little more about Thomas's own view of his art and artistry. First, he emphasized the importance of sound in his work. He said that *what the words stood for, symbolized, or meant was of very secondary importance, what mattered was the sound of them as I heard them for the first time on the lips of the remote and incomprehensible grown ups who seemed, for some reason, to be living in my world.*[54] Thomas described the effect words had on him: *the colours the words cast on my eyes ... and though what the words meant was to me in its own way, often deliciously funny enough, so much funnier seemed to me ... the shape and shade and size and noise of words as they hummed, strummed, jigged and galloped along. That was the time of innocence; words burst upon me, unencumbered by trivial or portentious association, words were their springlike selves, fresh with Eden's dew, as they flew out of the air.*[55]

But what of Swansea and West Wales in all this discussion about Thomas's poetry? Many poems have references to Swansea or have Swansea settings or associations. Sometimes the town is called simply *Tawe* or *Abertawe*, its Welsh name meaning 'the mouth of the River Tawe'. Such poems include *The Hunchback in the Park, Should Lanterns Shine, Once It Was the Colour of Saying, Especially When the October Wind, Greek Play in a Garden, Ears in the Turrets Hear, Why East Wind Chills, Poet, 1935, Rain Cuts the Place We Tread, Upon Your Hold - Out Hand, I have longed to move away and The Spire Cranes.* Many other poems come directly from West Wales or other parts of the Principality. *Over Sir John's Hill* is an obvious example but others not named refer to familiar landmarks or places such as, *We lying by seasand.* In a letter written in December, 1933, he pinpoints the inspiration for this poem: *I often go down in the mornings to the furthest point of Gower - the village of Rhossilli - and stay there until evening. The bay is the wildest, bleakest and barrenest I know - four or five miles of yellow coldness going away into the distance of the sea, And the Worm, a sea worm of rock pointing into the channel.*[56] Again in 1938 he took a nostalgic view of Swansea in *Once it was the colour of saying* which he called his Cwmdonkin (Park) poem. Earlier (9 May, 1932) he wrote about his childhood days in the same Park in *The Hunchback in the Park.*

We have already noted the importance of religion or Christian ethic in his work stemming from his Welsh upbringing. Others have mentioned the importance of the sea in Dylan's poetry. Kent Thompson in his unpublished Ph.D. thesis on *Dylan Thomas in Swansea* suggests that in the poet's imagination the sea was at once life and death and was the most powerful of all symbols for Thomas. It is rarely absent from his stories or poems. For anyone who spends his life in Swansea, the Gower and West Wales, the sea is all pervading and inescapable. 5 Cwmdonkin Drive faced the bay and when he was a boy and during his young days, Thomas haunted the foreshore. In later life, he lived in New Quay and Laugharne, again on the edge of the sea.

Finally, the symbolism in Thomas's poems and the whole panoply of metaphor, simile and other figures of speech and association are infused with this Welsh flavour. To mention only a few in different poems: *Men of nothing* in *I see the boys of summer* is an allusion to men in Corporation bathing suits in Swansea and again *Davy's lamp* in the same poem recalls the famous invention of Sir Humphrey Davy (especially important for Welsh miners). Dylan has a sly dig at his upbringing in *Our Eunuch dreams* where he mentions *Welshing*, that is decamping without paying. Glamorgan is mentioned twice in the poem *Hold hand, these ancient minutes*. Other Swansea and West Wales references are more oblique. For example, in the poem *Should lanterns shine*, Thomas mentions *Mummy cloths*. Gwen Watkins, the wife of Thomas's friend, Vernon, explained in *Portrait of a Friend* that this is a reference to a scene in *The Mummy's Claw* which Thomas and his friends had seen in the Uplands Cinema when they were mere youngsters. In *The Spire cranes*, Thomas was obviously thinking of the old ruined tower of Llanybri church and *a room with a stuffed fox and a stale fern* is said to be an accurate description of the front parlour of *Fern Hill Farm*. In *Poet: 1935*, Thomas makes a reference to 5 Cwmdonkin Drive:

Leaning from windows over a length
of lawns,
On tumbling hills admiring the sea

and in the *Notebooks* is a reference to Cwmdonkin Park:

I sit and mark
Love wet its arrow in the park.

There are, of course, numerous other references to this Park in which Thomas as a youngster spent so may happy hours:

The ball I threw while playing in the park
Has not yet reached the ground
(Should lanterns shine)

and

... I wheeled with mitching boys
through a resevoir park
... and stoned the cold and cuckoo lovers
(Once it was the colour of saying)

These few illustrations indicate the Welsh influence in Thomas's poetry. As for the prose, both his letters and his stories, these are redolent of Swansea, the Gower and West Wales. As far as his fiction is concerned, *Holiday Memory, Return Journey* and *The Followers* are all about Swansea. *A Child's Christmas in Wales* recalls his own life at 5 Cwmdonkin Drive whilst in *Adventures in the Skin Trade,* the first two parts of *A Fine Beginning* and *Portrait of the Artist as a Young Dog* (except for *A Visit to Grandpa's* and *Extraordinary Little Cough)* are all about Swansea. His other writings, *The Poems of Swansea* and *Reminiscences of Childhood* are similarly placed.

Thomas's memories of Gower as a young man appear in the *Portrait* stories. *Extraordinary Little Cough* and *Who Do You Wish Was With Us?* are examples. James A Davies in his book, *Dylan Thomas's Places* has listed 163 references to Swansea in the poet's work and many of these places are mentioned four or five times and in most cases more than twice.[57]

In Gower, Thomas mentions the Gower Cliffs, Bishopston, Fairwood Common, Llangennech, Mewslade, Oxwich, Pennard, Pwlldu Bay, Rhossilli and Worm's Head.[58]

Many of the places in Swansea have now disappeared. As Thomas said: *our Swansea is dead* but some of the people and places are still remembered affectionately by Swansea folk. Many, for example, will remember Ralph Wishart or 'Ralph the Books', the second-hand bookseller who knew Thomas and his mother well. Swansea is mentioned in Thomas's letters constantly and in his prose time after time. Writing to one of his drinking pals at Christmas, Thomas said that in Swansea he lived *a comfortable, sheltered, and now, only occasionally boozy life.*

Writing to Charles Fisher when away from the town in 1938 he affirmed *Swansea is still the best place* and that he would *set up ... in a neat villa full of drinks and pianos and lawnmowers and dumb-bells.* In December, 1939 from Laugharne he wrote again to Fisher about a Christmas visit to *our beautiful drab town* and declared he wanted *to hear the sweet town accent float into my ears like the noise of old brakes.* With Christmas, 1939 approaching he described Swansea as *his marble-town, city of laughter, little Dublin.* Cwmdonkin Drive, especially No. 5 is repeatedly mentioned in his correspondence and other writings. It is *the respectable Drive, a treed hill, field on one side, houses on the other,* or *the chilly glinting hill ... the seaward hill* of *A Child's Christmas in Wales* or the place *where the day ends* in *Holiday Memory.* From No. 5 he could hear *coughing sheep* which were the *plague* of his life (the sheep in the field opposite) and he described it variously as: *my nasty, provincial address, a provincial villa, a Glamorgan villa, a small, not very well painted, gateless house ... Very nice,very respectable and a mortgaged villa in an upper-class professional row.* It is No. 5 which is Samuel Bennet's home in *Mortimer Street (A Fine Beginning).* Thomas's interest in Swansea's dockland area is mirrored in his letters and prose. He told Pamela Hansford Johnson that he felt like throwing himself in [the dock] and he describes how he visited the pubs in the area with Mr. Farr *(Old Garbo).* In *Reminiscences of Childhood,* idlers watch ships sailing to and fro and in *Holiday Memory* he calls them *the sun-dazed docks round the corner of the sand-hills* and in *A Child's Christmas in Wales* he remembers the sounds of the seagulls from the docks. 38 Eversley Road, Sketty, the house called *Warmley* and the home of his lifelong friend, Daniel Jones, the celebrated Welsh musician, is recalled often by Thomas. *I still feel Warmley,* he wrote to Charles Fisher and later in another obvious pun, *I feel very Warmley to him all the time.* Almost the whole of the story, *The Fight* is set around *Warmley* and the name used, *Jenkyn* was Jones's middle name. The Mumbles is well documented in his work and so is the Uplands area. Thomas writes of *Mumbles* and *its oystered beer* and calls it *a rather nice village, despite its name.* In *Old Garbo,* he rcalls the place where *couples lay loving under their coats and looking at the Mumbles lighthouse.* The Uplands is described to Pamela Hansford Johnson as *a lowland collection of crossroads and shops.* Later in the same year (1934), he wrote to her of *A square, a handful of shops, a pub.* Whilst away, he recalls the place and vows when he returns he will be recognised by *his belly, black hat and a nostalgic flavour of the Uplands.*

Thomas was proud of the Gower and wrote to Pamela Hansford Johnson in December, 1933 describing it as *one of the loveliest sea-coast stretches in the whole of Britain* and again in 1934 he told her that he walked alone *over the very desolate Gower cliffs, communing with the cold and the quietness.* In *Who do You Wish Was With Us?* he described it as *the ash - white of the road, the common heathers, the green and blue of fields and fragmentary sea.* Finally, there is Rhossili the furthest point of the Gower peninsula. *The bay is the wildest, bleakest and barest I know* and when he is away he misses it greatly: *I wish I were in Rhossili.*

Any consideration of Dylan Thomas's work must include *Under Milk Wood.* However, the genesis of this *Play for Voices* is undoubtedly to be found in the writer's prose, *Out of my working ... came the idea that I write a piece, a play, an impression for voices, an entertainment out of the darkness, of the town I live in, and to write it simply and warmly and comically with lots of movement and varieties of moods, so that at many levels through sight and speech, descriptions and dialogue, vocation and parody, you came to know the town ...* [59] Above all, *Under Milk Wood* is important for its comedy - it is a parody of life in a Welsh seaside town. It gains from the fact that it is written almost entirely in direct speech.

In passing, it should be remembered that Thomas did not speak Welsh, and he did not consciously try to adopt Welsh forms. In *Under Milk Wood* he could not help taking a sly dig at sentimental Welshness

By Sawdde, Senny, Dovey, Dee,
Edw, Eden, Aled, all,
Taff and Towy broad and free,
Llyfnant with its waterfall,

Claerwen, Cleddau, Dulais, Daw,
Ely, Gwili, Ogwr, Nedd.
Small is our River Dewi, Lord,
A baby on a rushy bed.[60]

and follows this by making fun of Mrs. Ogmore Pritchard's cleanliness, Mr. Pugh's plotting and Mrs. Pugh's nagging. *Under Milk Wood* is an ideal world for it sees man's failures but helps us to laugh at them. Even the most reprehensible characters have something in their favour and there is nothing critical in his characterization of Polly Garter, the prostitute, or Cherry Owen, the town drunk. *And Polly Garter has many illegitimate babies but does not want only one man's. And Cherry Owen the soak, who likes getting drunk every night; and his wife who likes living with two men, one sober in the day, one drunk at night.*[61] As Professor Moynihan says, *'Under Milk Wood' has touches of great comedy* ... (he) ... *did not know that it would be his last work, but he could not have planned it better if he had. With all its incompleteness, its romantic and overblown rhetoric, its man-of-the-pub wit and fairy-tale timelessness, it summed up Thomas: the man and the work.*[62]

SOME THOUGHTS ON AMERICA

New York, *this titantic dream world, soaring Babylon ... this mad city ... the nightmare city.*

(Letter to his father and mother, 26 February, 1950.)

I said San Francisco was the best city on earth. It is incredibly beautiful, all hills and bridges and blinding blue sky and boats and the Pacific Ocean. (Letter to Caitlin, 5 April, 1950.)

Since I last wrote I have been in Florida, Winsconsin, Indiana, hell getting hotter all the time, I have been in Detroit, the worst city, the home of motor cars, and in and out of New York : But oh, San Francisco! It is and has everything ... Seafood is cheap. Chinese food is cheaper and lovely, and lovely California wine is good. The iced hock beer is good. What more? And the city is built on hills, it dances on the sun for nine months of the year, and the Pacific Ocean never runs dry.

(Letter to Caitlin 7 April, 1950.)

You asked me about the shops. I only know that the shops in the big cities in New York, Chicago, San Francisco, are full of everything you have heard of and also full of everything one has never heard of or seen.

(Letter to Caitlin, 7 April, 1950.)

I buried my head in the sands of America: flew over America like a damp, ranting bird; boomed and fiddled while home was burning. (Letter to Madame Caetani, 6 November, 1952.)

After the ulcerous rigours of a lecturer's spring, New York is a haven cosy as toast, cool as an icebox, and safe as skyscrapers. ... Boston where an audience might be *a bunch of dead pans and wealthy pots.* (from *Quite Early One Morning.*)

THE AMERICAN CONNECTION

Thomas was always fascinated with America and it is true to say that Americans have always been fascinated with him. An early indication of this interest is the fact that an American folk singer, Bob Zimmerman, so admired Dylan Thomas that he took the professional name of 'Bob Dylan'. On Broadway in the past there have been various productions of Brinnin's *Dylan Thomas in America* and Caitlin Thomas's *Leftover Life to Kill.* This shows the interest in him and his work in the USA.

It is clear that from 1945, Thomas was eager to go to America and he wrote frequently to Brinnin asking him to organise a visit. Brinnin prepared for his visit energetically and was willing to spend *big bucks* so that both men could prosper. Thomas thought the trip would be very worth while moneywise. He told James Laughlin, *With American money ... I won't, at once, have to chase again the hack-jobs by which, dear Christ, I live, have at once to set into motion again the insignificant, wheezy little machines that sausage out crumbs and coppers for me, scriplings, radio whinnies.*[63] Thus, it was that on 20th. February, 1950 he flew out to America and stayed there for 100 days.

Thomas enjoyed the experience overall but now and again he became tired of the travelling between the venues where he read his stories and poems. Brinnin had arranged talks and readings throughout the country. Thomas wrote to Caitlin from Ohio: *I never seem to sleep in a bed any more, only on planes and trains. I'm hardly living; I'm just a voice on wheels. And the damndest thing is that quite likely I may arrive home with hardly any money at all, both the United States and Great Britain taxing any earnings - my earnings for us, Colum, Aeronwy, Llewelyn, for our house that makes me cry to think of, for the water, the heron, old and empty Brown's ...*[64] Martin E. Gingerich in a lecture he gave to The Dylan Thomas Society Wales Branch in March, 1978 outlined the number of miles Dylan travelled on his American trips. On the first visit he had a 17 hour plane trip from Britain, and after two appearances Brinnin drove him 100 miles to new Haven, Connecticut. Two days later he went by train the 100 miles to Boston and the following day he was driven a further 100 miles to Mount Holyoke. In about two weeks he had travelled 1000 miles. Gingerich then outlines the distances Thomas travelled in the rest of his first tour.

New York to Chicago (725 miles), stopping to read in western New York State and Ohio.
Chicago to South Bend, Indiana (75 miles).
To Urbana, Illinois, and on to Iowa City (400 miles). All this was by train.
By air to San Francisco (1,500 miles), Tuesday, 4th. April.
By train to Vancouver, Canada (800 miles), 6th. April.
Back to the United States to Seattle, Washington (125 miles).
To Los Angeles, California (950 miles). All this by train.
After eight days in the Los Angeles area reading at various universities, Dylan flew back to New York (about 3,000 miles) where he spent three days in the city, after which he was driven about a hundred miles upstate to Hobart in Geneva, New York.[65]

By the end of the tour, Thomas was exhausted. He wrote to his parents on 22 May, 1950 (he left the USA on the 31st.): *At last my tour is at an end. I have visited over forty universities, schools and colleges, from Vancouver, in British Columbia, to southern Florida. I have travelled right through the Middle West, the North West, and on to the western coast of California. It has been the time element in this tour that has been the most tiring ... I have almost never had a moment to myself, except in bed and then I was too exhausted to do anything. And the varying kinds of climates and temperatures have lessened my energy, too. In Chicago, it was bitterly snowing: a few days later, in Florida, the temperature was ninety. And New York itself never has the same sort of weather 2 days running.*[66]

In all, Thomas made four visits to the USA.

The first (outlined above) from 21 February, 1950 to 31 May, 1950.
The second with his wife, Caitlin, from 20 January, 1952 to 16 May, 1952.
The third from 21 April 1953 to 3 June, 1953.
And the fourth from 19 October 1953 to 9 November, 1953.

Tragically, visit four ended with Thomas's death in New York.

Gingerich analyses the three visits from a money point of view and argues that *Dylan went to the United States to ease his money worries and to eliminate his most pressing debts to free himself for his writing.* But after three visits: *He left the United States not only still worried by debts, but also completely exhausted and broken in health. It is sadly ironic that in four years after his death, Dylan's works earned two million dollars.*[67]

The four visits gave Thomas an international reputation as a poet, a raconteur, a first class reader in public and a lecturer. Unfortunately, it also added to his reputation for scandalous behaviour.

There is no doubt that Thomas liked the United States, particularly New York, and he enjoyed the bonhomie of the Americans. At first the whole country was a little overwhelming but he became very fond of the Greenwich and Chelsea village areas of New York and drank regularly at the White Horse Tavern on Hudson Street. On the first visit he lived near Washington Square and on the second and third in rooms at the Chelsea Hotel. Paul Ferris has pointed out the significance of his attraction to this particular part of New York: its proximity to the wharves of the Hudson River struck a chord in Thomas's mind. It reminded him of the docks area in pre-war Swansea.

Thomas certainly felt he was appreciated in the USA. In one of his letters to Brinnin he wrote (18 March, 1953) just before his third visit, that in the USA he found *appreciation, dramatic work and friends.* He argued *after the ulcerous rigours of a lecturer's spring, New York is a haven cosy as toast, cool as an icebox, and safe as skyscrapers.*

There have always been arguments about where Thomas wrote *Under Milk Wood,* the town or village on which it is based and who the characters were based on. The answer is, of course, that these arguments are irrelevant. *Under Milk Wood* is timeless and is based on a variety of characters: they are an amalgam of Welsh life and character, a caricature. New Quay, Ferryside or Laugharne, it does not mattter, the characters live on in the mind and imagination. Many do not realize that his *Play for Voices* was actually completed during his third trip to America. Paul Ferris recounts the events leading to its first performance at the Poetry Center in New York on 14 May, 1953. *It was finally put together, with some makeshift passages, less than an hour before the curtain rose in New York... Soon the audience realised that they were hearing a romantic comedy and responded accordingly. Thomas was exporting a caricature, the sad and comical Welsh in their potty little village; many of the real Welsh bridled when they heard it later from the B.B.C. taking special offence at the bawdy passages.*[68] Ferris argues that the only reason Thomas finished the play was that the Americans were willing to pay for it.

The Americans have sustained their interest in Thomas and his work. His material continues to be published in the USA by New Directions, his tapes, many of which originated in America (produced by Caedman Records) still continue to be popular there. There is a steady stream of Americans who come to Swansea and Laugharne to see where the poet lived and worked and to visit the simple graves in Laugharne. It is no wonder that much of the material on Thomas belongs to learned institutions in the USA. For example, the Harry Ransom Humanities Research Center of the University of Texas at Austin has the largest collection of Thomas's letters and the Poetry and Rare Books Collection of the Library of the State University of New York at Buffalo treasures his letters to Pamela Hansford Johnson and the Thomas *Notebooks*.

Finally, those in high places have long admired the poet's work. Jimmy Carter, 39th. President of the USA believed that Thomas should be recognised nationally and internationally. He was concerned that the poet was not represented in Poet's Corner in Westminster Abbey and it is largely through the President's efforts that Thomas now has a place there amongst other great British poets.

In his recently published first book of poems, *Always a Reckoning,* President Carter has included a poem that he wrote about Thomas's recognition at Westminster Abbey. With the President's permission the poem is reproduced in this book.

A President Expresses Concern on a Visit to Westminster Abbey

Poet's Corner had no epitaph
to mark the Welshman's
sullen art or craft
because, they said,
his morals were below
the standards there.
I mentioned the ways of Poe
and Byron,
and the censored Joyce's works;
at least the newsmen listened,
noted my remarks
and his wife, Caitlin, wrote.
We launched a clumsy, weak campaign,
the bishops met
and listened to the lilting lines again.
Later, some Welshmen brought to me
a copy of the stone
that honors now the beauty he set free
from a godhead of his own.

Dylan by Alfred Janes

THE DYLAN THOMAS LEGACY

During his lifetime (and since his death) Dylan Thomas was and is one of the most controversial writers of modern literature. A whole series of writers and critics have considered his life and work. Some, as we have seen, argued that Thomas was a deeply religious poet: others have disagreed. Some have said the poems are the most carefully contrived ever written: others *that they are a meaningless hot sprawl of mud.* Dylan wrote to Vernon Watkins that: *I admit that readers of complicated poetry do need a breather now and them, but I don't think that the poet should give it to them.* One of the most critical of Thomas's work is David Holbrook and he has described the poet's work as immature. *He only had a few things to say* and *he said these badly*. His work *yields no feeling of achieved pattern or structure*. This criticism has been followed by others, notably George Steiner. On the other hand, Herbert Read has said of Dylan's work, it is *the most absolute poetry ... written in our time* and T H Jones has argued that by 1946 Dylan *had developed into a serious and mature artist in beautiful control of his rhythms, images and his words.* David Daiches has also noted the supreme artistry of Thomas's work in *The Poetry of Dylan Thomas.* The controversies continue.

The work of Dylan Thomas has inspired the genius of others. Records and tapes made by the poet have been on sale since his death and the first stage production of *Under Milk Wood* and much of his B.B.C. work has been re-broadcast. Thomas has inspired a great deal of written material. His wife, Caitlin, wrote two books called *Leftover Life to Kill* (1957) and *Not Quite Posthumous Letters to My Daughter*. Thomas has also inspired literary collectors all over the world and any scrap of paper which can be identified as coming from his pen has found a market: there is always someone who wants to buy.

Thomas's poetry has been set to music. First, there was Daniel Jones who delighted in using his friend's poetry as a vehicle for his music and there have been others who used his life and work for musical purposes.

We have mentioned already that a number of plays have been written about the poet. In London and on Broadway there have, for example, been various productions of *Dylan Thomas in America* and *Leftover Life to Kill* inspired by the books of John Malcolm Brinnin and Caitlin Thomas. Rock legend Mick Jagger is to produce a movie about the life of Dylan and Caitlin. The movie will be written and directed by Christopher Monger, director of the latest Hugh Grant film, *The Englishman Who Went up a Hill But Came Down a Mountain.* Jagger says: *Dylan Thomas and Caitlin's relationship was so volatile and intense that I knew as soon as I read the book that it would make a great film.* Monger will adapt the movie from the book, *Caitlin: Life with Dylan Thomas,* written by his wife and Geoge Tremlett.

When he was alive, artists delighted in painting the poet and there are pictures of him by Augustus John, Alfred Janes, Mervyn Levy and Ceri Richards and posthumously other artists are painting new portraits.[69] His work has also inspired another art form. This began when he was alive and was devised by the late W. Emlyn Davies who lived at 5 Cwmdonkin Drive after the Thomas's had left it. Mr. Davies saw in the poems a medium for his own self-expression and devised calligrams on the poet's work. These calligrams *illuminate* the work of the poet and in them he found a new way for us to see several dimensions of meaning at one and the same time. Gretchen Holstein Schoff of the University of Wisconsin comments on these calligrams thus: *I realised almost immediately that the illuminations were a unique commentary on some of the most perplexing and haunting poems in the English languge. Here, in colours, involuted patterns of words, visual fantasies, were the images literary critics ... struggle to explicate in flat, black and white prose. Critics of Thomas are perpetually vexed in their efforts to 'make sense' out of poems that 'make metasense'. And it never works, completely. Between the stroke of the poet's pen and the clack of the critic's typewriter falls the shadow. We solemnly take a phrase like 'singing light' and try out its connotations and deviations, reading 'light' as noun and then as modifier. We inch toward a kind of truth in a strung out series of 'possibilities of meaning'. And in the process the magic is lost. I have tried for a long time, and predictably in vain, to pinpoint the sleight-of-hand in Thomas's poems, that peculiar density of evocation in which his images seem to have layer after layer of simultaneous and interlocking meanings.* She goes on to say that *Emlyn Davies has found, in these illuminations, a new way for us to see several dimensions of meaning at one and the same time. The 'simultaneous evocation' that eludes the conventional critic ... is in the illuminations. It seems to me that we are able to experience a kind of aesthetic holography, where simply by moving our heads slightly to right or left our entire perception of what we see takes on depth ... The world has all too few visionaries - those rare men who see by special light. The Illuminations reveal the possibility of human communion between two artists. Both of them laboured by 'singing light'.*

A Calligram by Emlyn Davies

Dylan Thomas was himself fascinated by this work and wrote the following letter to Emlyn Davies in April, 1946:

Holywell Ford
Oxford
April ~~March~~ 26th 1946

Dear Emlyn Davies,

What a wonderful gift. A very very lovely book, eye-and-I-delighting, and, to me, a great tribute. I shall always keep and treasure it. Dent's didn't send it along until last week, and then I was away. I came back to find this burningly good present waiting. Dent's had kept it in their office for days, to show everyone; they wrote to tell me, as indeed they ~~should~~ write to tell you, however well you must know it, what a splendid piece of craftsmanship they thought it was, and how much everyone there appreciated it. No-one can appreciate it as I do, except perhaps my children when they're old enough. And no, they couldn't either.

Of course I remember you, and well, though it was such a short friendship owing to all kinds of reasons — mostly, I think (and hope) to my going away. It's strange to think of you living in the house where I was born. If I come to Swansea, as I certainly shall do one day, though, as you probably know, my mother and father are now in Carmarthenshire and I have very few home associations in the town, may I call and see you?

A very good friend of mine lives in
Swansea; he's just returned after five and a
bit years in the Air Force: Vernon Watkins.
Do you know him? I'm sure you know some of
his poems. He lives at 131 Glanmor Road,
Sketty. If you don't know him, I wish you
would. I'm writing to him, and may I
give him your address too? He has great
powers and profound poetical sincerity, an
ear for all music and a tongue against
all humbug: he's a pretty marvellous
chap, but don't tell him I said so.

It would be silly to say that I'm
glad you like my poems; glad's a spindly
little world, and there is no such thing
as 'like' in the splendidly loving care
of your beautiful penmanship. But I am
glad, anyway. Glad that you remember that
evening, years ago, in Cwmdonkin Drive. Glad to
think that the first printed poem of mine, Light
Breaks, must have said to you what it meant
to me.

My wife, whose name is Caitlin, wants to say
with me again: Thank you for the book.

All good wishes,

Yours,

Dylan Thomas.

Hand-crafted mural in ceramics from the Bryn Melyn Studio of Llanelltyd

As well as this written tradition, Dylan Thomas inspired other work, most of which has been carried out posthumously. Ceri Richards met Thomas only once but was moved to draw and paint because of his work. Thus, *The Black Apple of Gower*, an oil painting, and a watercolour entitled, *The force that through the green fuse* are only two of the many items this artist painted during Thomas's lifetime. Others include *Illustration to a Poem by Dylan Thomas*, a lithograph, *Homage to Dylan Thomas*, a watercolour and *Design for a drop cloth*, a Gouache. After Thomas's death, Richards drew twelve lithographs on poems by Dylan Thomas and a pen and water colour illustration entitled, *The Poet's Prologue*. In 1984, the Gregynog Press published a limited edition of Thomas's *Deaths and Entrances* which included a series of colour prints by the artist John Piper. In 1990, Ruth Jen Ifans painted a striking cover for a book in Welsh which was loosely based on the life of the poet. Peter Blake of Libanus Press in Marlborough is working on a series of wood-cuts to be used in a special edition of *Under Milk Wood*. A preview of this work in progress is featured in the Dylan Thomas Exhibition at the National Literature Centre in Swansea throughout 1995.

The tradition has also been followed by craftsmen throughout Wales. For example, in recent years the Bryn Melyn Studio of Llanelltyd, Dolgellau in Gwynedd has created a hand-crafted mural in ceramics. Their comments on the collection are: *Humble terraced dwellings, built for sailboat fishermen over 100 years ago, form the body and soul of the village. Here lived Mr. and Mrs. Floyd, Ocky Milkman, Evans the Death, Mr. Waldo and many more of Dylan Thomas's unforgettable characters. At the heart of the village are the shops of Mog Edwards, Butcher Beynon, Mrs. Organ Morgan, Myfanwy Price. Here also is the chapel, Bethesda; the school the Sailors Arms, the Welfare Hall and the Town Clock. We have created all these using our deep knowledge and love of 'Under Milk Wood' and of Dylan Thomas's home village in Wales. It is for you to complete the re-creation of Dylan's dream village as you believe it to have been.*

The tradition has been maintained in Laugharne and his home town of Swansea. The former has become a shrine to our national poet. The *Boat House* has undergone conversion from a home into a museum. Now in the ownership of Carmarthen District Council the four-square exterior has been completely repaired. The walls have been painted white once again and the woodwork has been repainted a bright, light blue. The wooden verandah and steps have been renewed. The sunken garden in front of the house has been paved over. The Local Authority have an information office inside the *Boat House* and the museum has numerous exhibits including photographs of Thomas and his family and facsimiles of his manuscripts. There are also audio-visual materials and regular film shows. The former are in foreign languages as well as English. Poetry readings and small-scale performances are encouraged and every year Laugharne actors, the Llaregyb Players, recreate Dylan's work for the increasing number of visitors.

In recent years Swansea City has done much to foster the Dylan Thomas tradition. A plaque on the front of 5 Cwmdonkin Drive indicates where the poet was born and there are statues of both Thomas and one of the characters of *Under Milk Wood* (Captain Cat) on the new Marina. More recently, the city fathers have rebuilt and renovated a literature centre in the 'old' dockland area. This is now the Dylan Thomas Centre which has hosted a major Dylan Thomas Exhibition as part of the celebrations for the UK Year of Literature.

The rich legacy of Dylan Thomas lives and continues to develop, an inspiration to us all.

LINKS WITH DYLAN THOMAS
- SWANSEA AND WEST WALES TODAY

Much of the Swansea that Thomas knew still exists - certainly the memory of the poet and his work lives on. These photographs are to remind people of his life and work and the beauty of the places he loved.

DYLAN THOMAS'S BIRTHPLACE
5 Cwmdonkin Drive

This is the house where the poet was born, a comfortable semi on a hill conveniently near the Uplands shopping centre and Cwmdonkin Park. From the top of the house, young Thomas could see the sweep of Swansea Bay as far as the Mumbles. Little wonder that he loved the sea.

Thomas had a happy childhood. His mother doted on him and in a letter to Pamela Hansford Johnson he explained that it was possible to have *a too-happy childhood.* In another letter to her he described the house as *a small, not very well-painted, gateless house ... very nice, very respectable.* As if embarrassed by his affection for the place, he referred to it in other correspondence and in his work as a *provincial villa; a Glamorgan villa* and a *mortgaged villa in an upper-class professional row.*

Thomas lived at No. 5 until 10 November, 1934. Then, he left home for the first time to live in London. Never really happy away from Wales, he came home several times between March 1935 to February, 1937. In April, 1937 his parents sold the house and moved to Bishopston. Today, the house is still in private hands. The blue plaque on the wall commemorates the poet.

DYLAN
THOMAS
POET
1914-1953
was born in
this house

THE SECRET WORLD OF CWMDONKIN PARK

This was where the young Dylan had fun with his friends, a private world in which they played out their fantasies and childhood adventures. Very near the poet's home, it is mentioned time and again in his work. Thomas was very happy there and he thought of it as one of Swansea's best features.

... I whistled with mitching boys
through a reservoir park
... and stoned the cold cuckoo
lovers
(Once it was the colour of saying)

The reservoir has now disappeared.

He describes Cwmdonkin Park in *Reminiscences of Childhood* as *a world within the world of the sea town, full of terrors and treasures ... a country just born and always changing.*

CWMDONKIN PARK

This is the fountain in Cwmdonkin Park. The Park was the main subject of his poem, *The Hunchback in the Park*, and Thomas refers to

... the fountain basin where I sailed my ship

Once there were chained iron drinking cups to take the water but these have been replaced by a push-button tap. In his work, the poet clung to his childhood, unwilling or unable to leave the happy memories. Time and again he includes Cwmdonkin in his poems:

the star-gestured children in the park
(Especially when the October wind)

and

The ball I threw while playing in the park
Has not reached the ground
(Should lanterns shine)

MEMORIAL TO A POET

In 1963, the last three lines from *Fern Hill* were inscribed on this large stone in Cwmdonkin Park.

... Oh as I was young and easy in the mercy of his means,
Time held me green and dying
Though I sang in my chains like the sea.

The stone was cut as a tribute to the poet.

Oh as I was young and easy in the mercy of his means
time held me green and dying
though I sang in my chains like the sea
DYLAN THOMAS

UPLANDS, SWANSEA

In Thomas's day, this was a middle-class residential suburb of Swansea with a few select shops. 5 Cwmdonkin Drive is about five minutes away.

Nowadays, the Uplands is a busy shopping centre complete with supermarket and fast food diner, dominated by the car. The Uplands Cinema, the 'flea pit' is now an up-market branch of Lloyds Bank and Mrs Ferguson's sweet shop where he used to buy his wine gums and later, Woodbines, disappeared several years ago. But the Uplands Hotel, Thomas's local where he used to drink with his friends is still there. In recent years, it has concentrated on themes and the poet would have been amused to learn that he was 'a theme' and is now 'a Dylan's snug bar'.

Thomas mentions the Uplands frequently in his letters and in his work. To Pamela Hansford Johnson he calls it *a lowland collection of shops* (January, 1934) and *A square, a handful of shops, a pub* (July, 1934).

'£1' SPORTS
M369 LWN

SWANSEA

This is a bird's eye view of the City of Swansea today showing how it has spread towards the sea. It is very different from the *ugly, lovely town ... crawling, sprawling, slummed, unplanned* of *Reminiscences of Childhood.* To the right is the comparatively new, impressive County Hall and on the extreme left is a glimpse of Swansea docks. Much of this area would have been visible from the top of 5 Cwmdonkin Drive but the landscape has changed considerably: the number of houses and buildings has grown since the 1930s.

Thomas loved Swansea and as late as December, 1939, he described it as *his marble town, city of laughter, little Dublin...*

SWANSEA SANDS

This is a view of the beach, with the tide out, at Swansea. It is a large beach stretching for miles from Swansea Docks in the west to the Mumbles in the east. There is plenty of room for young boys to build castles, play quoits and football. At other times it is a serene place, ideal for walking. On a sunny day, it compares favourably with beaches anywhere.

This photograph has been taken in the part of Swansea sands nearest the town at a place called the 'Slip'. In Thomas's day, this was a good place for a day out with the children and family. Thomas described the sands on August Bank Holiday in his story, *Holiday Memory.*

Nearby is the Promenade, a favourite place for walks especially on fine Sunday evenings. Almost opposite is St. Helen's where the poet often went *to sit in the sun and watch a county cricket match.*

SWANSEA MARINA

Located in Swansea Marina, this statue shows Thomas looking out over the docks to the sea. This is a young Dylan in contemplation. Nearby, is a statue of Captain Cat, one of his most famous characters from *Under Milk Wood.*

The sea was important to the poet and is a recurring image in his work. The hardback chair is similar to the one he used in his Work Hut at Laugharne.

TŶ LLÊN
THE DYLAN THOMAS CENTRE

Built on the site of the Old Guildhall, this is the only purpose-built literature centre in the United Kingdom. It was opened by Thomas's daughter, Aeronwy, in 1995. Swansea is host to the Year of Literature and this Centre is a fitting memorial to the poet.

The Centre houses a varied programme of literary events including book launches, exhibitions and lectures. There is a writers' workshop, a gift shop and a bookshop. It has a restaurant and bar and can cater for conferences.

THE DYLAN THOMAS CENTRE
1995
CANOLFAN DYLAN THOMAS

THE MUMBLES LIGHTHOUSE

This view of the lighthouse is little changed. It can be reached by foot at low tide (but the currents of the incoming tide are dangerous here). Thomas loved the Mumbles, full of fishing and sailing boats, pubs, amusements and a pier. It has a magical attraction: narrow winding streets and tree-lined lanes, whitewashed cottage walls and noisy, diving seagulls. The weather is not always kind but visitors return year after year.

Young Thomas often stayed with his Aunt Dosie who had married a clergyman in nearby Newton, just a stone's throw from another glorious bay, Caswell. His Aunt spoiled him. Little wonder he did not want to leave his childhood behind.

The tram has gone, the road linking the Mumbles with Swansea has been widened and is always crowded with cars, the ice cream parlour is bigger but the village has kept its identity and wisely resisted change and the developers.

Thomas described it to Pamela Hansford Johnson as *a rather nice village despite its name* and in *Holiday Memory*, he affectionately called it, *Mumbles where the aunties grew*.

THE ANTELOPE, MUMBLES

This is one of the pubs that Thomas used to frequent with his friends. It was conveniently close to the Little Theatre and whilst rehearsing, the poet often went there for a quick pint. It was this habit that eventually lost him the leading role in one of the plays.

To the poet, pubs were not merely places where he went to drink. They were sociable places where he could meet his friends, catch up with local gossip and enjoy lively conversation. A pub meant warmth, company and entertainment. Thomas always loved to be the centre of attraction and it has been said that the poet would have been a lonely, solitary man without the camaraderie and bonhomie of the Welsh pub.

The Antelope
COURAGE
EST. 1787
VILLAGE LANE

THREE CLIFFS BAY, GOWER

One of the many bays on the Gower peninsula visited by Thomas. He mentions the Gower and the bays in his poetry, prose and letters. Writing to Pamela Hansford Johnson, he described the area as *one of the loveliest sea-coast stretches in the whole of Britain.*

This aerial photograph of Three Cliffs Bay captures its beauty. The influence of the sea, the grandeur of sea carved cliffs, the contrast between sandy beaches and green countryside flowed through Thomas's imagination and his work.

WORM'S HEAD

This is the part of Gower Thomas loved best. Worm's Head, a mile-long, sticks out into the sea, a desolate rock, resting place for sea birds and those that dare the tides to reach it when the sea is out. Thomas often walked it with his friends revelling in the battle between the wind and sea. The bay is Rhossilli, the furthest point on the Gower peninsula, five miles of golden sand overshadowed by huge cliffs.

Thomas described the bay as *the wildest, bleakest and barrenest I know*. In *Who do You Wish Was With Us?* he described being marooned on the Worm when he and Ray Price were cut off by the tide.

NEW QUAY, WEST WALES

This is a view of New Quay showing its cliff top appearance looking out to the sea. Thomas lived here from September, 1944 until the summer of 1945. *The toppling town* as he called it was part of his inspiration for *Under Milk Wood.* Thomas used New Quay as the subject for one of his verse letters and the place was featured in the story, *Quite Early One Morning.* But he was unhappy at this time. This may have been because he was out of funds. He wrote to Vernon Watkins (21 May, 1945) that *I am broke and depressed and have just returned from London and hated it more than ever and though it is lovely here I am not.*

LAUGHARNE, WEST WALES

This picture shows the middle of Laugharne in West Wales. The Town Hall is in the foreground and Dylan's comment about it to Margaret Taylor was that *its clock tells the time backwards*. Thomas would have passed the Town Hall on his way to Brown's Hotel in the main street.

Laugharne was home for the Thomas family from April, 1949 until the poet died on 9 November, 1953. In this quiet, gentle place where change is never in fashion, the poet could work far away from the hustle and bustle of city life. It was the setting for many of his poems including *When I woke, Over Sir John's Hill,* and more importantly *Under Milk Wood.*

BROWN'S HOTEL, LAUGHARNE

In the middle of town, this was Thomas's favourite pub when he lived in Laugharne. He walked to it daily as part of his normal routine. During the poet's time it was owned by the Williams family, the local entrepreneurs. They ran and owned the local buses, the local taxis, the diesel generators that provided the town with electricity and they also owned *Sea View* which the Thomas family rented for a time. The poet came to know Ebi Williams and his wife, Joy well. When he was away, Thomas mentioned this pub in his letters. It was a place he wanted to return to, a place where he felt safe among friends.

BROWN'S HOTEL
BROWN'S HOTEL
FREE

SEA VIEW, LAUGHARNE

One of several homes the Thomas family rented in Laugharne: the house with four storeys is near the Castle. The family lived there from July, 1938 to July, 1940. At this time there was no electricity in the house and candles in beer bottles were used to light their evenings. Vernon Watkins said that this time at *Sea View* was one of the happiest for the poet.

LAUGHARNE CASTLE

An idyllic view of the Castle at Laugharne, *the castle Brown as owls* of *Poem in October* and the *collapsed castle* of *The Crumbs of One Man's Year* .

A Georgian house adjoining this Castle was rented by the Welsh author, Richard Hughes. The Thomas family stayed there for a few months from April, 1941 to August 1941 whilst Hughes was away during the war. The poet worked in the gazebo and wrote part of *Portrait of the Artist as a Young Dog* there. According to Ferris, Thomas told Vernon Watkins: *I have the romantic, dirty summerhouse looking over the marsh to write in ...* and *Caitlin an almost empty, large room to dance in.*

THE BOAT HOUSE, LAUGHARNE

This is another view of the *Boat House* (see front cover). It shows the house and estuary below. It was the home of the Thomas family from April/May 1949 until his death on 9 November, 1953.

Whilst the family was here, the youngest boy was born. He was named Colum Garan, (Garan is the Welsh for Heron). The *Boat House* was bought for them by Margaret Taylor and they paid her a peppercorn rent.

The location seems to be idyllic for a writer but unfortunately, Thomas had a weak chest and there were problems for him especially during the long, cold and damp winters. Writing to Madame Caetani on 6 November, 1952, Thomas expressed his feelings about the *Boat House* which was then in a poor state of repair: *this tumbling house whose every broken pane and wind-whipped-off slate, childscrawled wall, rain-stain, mousehole, knobble and ricket, man-booby-and-rat-trap, I know in my sleep.*

THOMAS'S WORK-HUT, LAUGHARNE

This is the Work-Hut or shed above the *Boat House* at Laugharne which was the poet's study. It overlooks the estuary and has a beautiful view of the bay. The Hut has been renovated and the plaque near it gives details of what it was used for. Visitors to the *Boat House* can peer through the window to see inside.

It is not clear how much work Thomas did in the Hut but he wrote several of his poems here including *Over St John's Hill* which he could see from his window. He described the work-hut in different ways. To Madame Caetani in November, 1952, he called it *my wordsplashed hut* and in *Poem on his Birthday,* it became

the long tongued room
... his slant, racking house.

INSIDE THE WORK-HUT, LAUGHARNE

This picture shows the inside of Thomas's study supposedly just as he left it with his work table facing the window and the estuary. Note the scripts on the table and the crumpled papers discarded on the floor. Note also the rickety chairs, evidence of the poverty of the poet. There are just a few books - a dictionary and thesaurus, part of his essential equipment.

In his book, *Dylan Thomas in America,* John Malcolm Brinnin described the Hut as *The Studio, which Dylan called the shack ... was a rat's nest of chewed, rolled and discarded papers - piles of manuscripts, unanswered (often unopened) letters, empty cigarette packages, small stacks of literary periodicals, tradesmen's bills and publishers brochures. Snatches of poetry lay under empty beer bottles. Volumes of poetry mouldered where they had been placed months, years before. Besides a single table and two straight-backed chairs, the studio contained three or four half-filled cartons of books ...*

One wonders if, during his visit, Brinnin looked out of the window.

THE GRAVES OF DYLAN THOMAS AND CAITLIN, LAUGHARNE

A simple cross marks the grave of Dylan Thomas at St. Martin's Church, Laugharne. The poet was buried here on 24 November, 1953. The inscription on the white wooden cross reads

In
Memory
of
Dylan Thomas
Died Nov 9
1953
R I P

Below this cross is a stone inscribed *Caitlin*. Dylan and the love of his life are at peace together.

In memory of
Dylan Thomas
died Nov 9 1953
RIP
IN LOVING MEMORY OF
Gertrude Elizabeth Williams,
DAUGHTER OF ALDERMAN MAURICE
AND LILIAN GERTRUDE WILLIAMS
ALSO
ALDERMAN Ernest Vincent Williams,
ORGANIST AND CHOIRMASTER OF ST MARTIN'S CHURCH
BORN JANUARY 22. 1896.
DIED FEBRUARY 9. 1964.

BRIEF CHRONOLOGY

27 Oct. 1914	Dylan Marlais Thomas born in Swansea at 5 Cwmdonkin Drive.
Sept. 1925	Entered Swansea Grammar School where his father taught English.
	First published poem, *The Song of the Mischievous Dog*.
27 April, 1930	Started the first of the *Notebooks* into which he copied his early poems.
	These *Notebooks* continued until April, 1934.
July, 1931	Left School.
Sept. 1931	Became a reporter on the *South Wales Daily Post* (later the *South Wales Evening Post*). He was 16.
Nov. 1932	Left *Evening Post*.
March 1933	First poem published in London: *And death shall have no dominion* appeared in the *New English Weekly*.
Aug. 1933	First visited London.
Sept. 1933	First poem *(That Sanity be Kept)* published in the 'Poet's Corner' section of the *Sunday Referee*.
	Correspondence with Pamela Hansford Johnson began.
22 April, 1934	Won the Book Prize of 'Poet's Corner' which meant his first collection of poems was sponsored by the *Sunday Referee*.
March - Nov. 1934	Visited London several times.
10 Nov, 1934	Moved to London.
10 Dec. 1934	*18 Poems* published.
April, 1936	Met Caitlin Macnamara.
11 Sept. 1936	*Twenty-five Poems* published.

11 July, 1937	Married Caitlin Macnamara.
21 April, 1937	First broadcast *(Life and the Modern Poet).*
May, 1938	First moved to live in Laugharne.
30 Jan. 1939	First child, a son, Llewelyn, born in Hampshire.
24 Aug. 1939	*The Map of Love* consisting of poetry and stories published.
20 Dec. 1939	*The World I Breathe,* a selection of his poetry and prose published. (First volume publication in America.)
4 April, 1940	*Portrait of the Artist as Young Dog* (short stories) published.
July, 1940	Left Laugharne for London.
Sept. 1940	Began work as a film script-writer for the Strand Film Company.
1940 - 1942	Lived partly in London and partly in Wales.
1942	Wife and child went to live with him in Chelsea, London.
March, 1943	Birth of his second child, a daughter, Aeronwy, in London.
1943	Started to have regular broadcasting work.
Sept. 1944 to Summer 1945	Lived at New Quay.
Summer 1945 to spring 1946	Lived in London.
7 Feb. 1946	*Deaths and Entrances* published.
March, 1946 to May, 1949	Lived in or near Oxford.
8 Nov. 1946	*Selected Writings* published in USA.
April - Aug. 1947	Visited Italy.
Sept. 1947	Moved to South Leigh, Oxfordshire.
1948	Wrote feature films for Gainsborough.
March, 1949	Visited Prague as a guest of the Czechoslovak government.
May, 1949	Returned to Laugharne and lived in the *Boat House.*
July, 1949	Birth of his second son, Colum.

Feb. - June, 1950	First American tour.
Jan. 1951	Went to Iran to write a film script for the Anglo Iranian Oil Company.
Jan.- May, 1952	Second American tour.
Feb. 1952	*In Country Sleep* published in America.
10 Nov. 1952	*Collected Poems* published.
15 Dec. 1952	Thomas's father died.
31 March, 1953	*Collected Poems* published in the USA.
April - June, 1953	Third American tour.
14 May, 1953	First performance of *Under Milk Wood* in New York.
	The Doctor and the Devils: the first of the film scripts to be published.
Oct. 1953	Left Wales for his fourth American tour.
9 Nov. 1953	Died in St. Vincent's Hospital, New York City.
1954	*Under Milk Wood* published.

REFERENCES AND NOTES

[1]*The Mabinogion.*

[2]Paul Ferris, *Dylan Thomas,* Penguin Books, 1977, p. 22 - 3.

[3]Letter to Pamela Hansford Johnson, 15 October, 1933. Thomas also explained in his letter that Dylan meant *the prince of darkness.*

[4]*Reminiscences of Childhood.* First version.

[5]*Reminiscences of Childhood* and *Return Journey, Quite Early One Morning,* pp. 13 - 14.

[6]This event is recorded by both Ferris in his *Dylan Thomas* and in Thompson's Ph.D. thesis, *Dylan Thomas in Swansea.*

[7]Op. cit, Ferris, p. 37.

[8]*Reminiscences of Childhood.*

[9]Ibid.

[10]Ibid.

[11]This story is repeated in both Ferris's work and in Thompson's thesis.

[12]*Swansea Grammar School Magazine,* Vol. 26, No. 2, July 1929 p. 54.
Sea also Vol. 27 No.1, December, 1930 p. 97.

[13]A picture about his feat was published in the *Cambrian Daily Leader,* September, 1925.

[14]Mervyn Levy, *A Womb with a View,* John O'London's weekly, 26 November, 1962 p. 485.

[15]Bill Read, *The Days of Dylan Thomas*, p. 34.

[16]Op. cit., Ferris.

[1]The Narrator in *Return Journey.*

[18]Ibid.

[19]Ibid.

[20]Article about Llewellyn Pritchard by Thomas in the *Herald of Wales,* 23 January, 1932.

[21]*Quite Early One Morning.*

[22]*Portrait of the Artist as a Young Dog.*

[23]Letter to Trevor Hughes, July, 1933.

[24]Letter to Pamela Hansford Johnson, October, 1933.

[25]*Who Do You Wish Was Was With Us?*

[26]This letter quoted by Paul Ferris, pp. 72 - 73.

[27]Ibid.

[28]Ibid, p. 75.

[29]Op. cit., Bill Read, p. 47.

[30]Letter to Trevor Hughes, January, 1933.

[31]*South Wales Evening Post,* February, 1934.

[32]See Peter Stead, *The Swansea of Dylan Thomas* in *Dylan Thomas Remembered,* pp. 13 onwards.

[33]Letter to Pamela Hansford Johnson, January, 1934.

[34]Letter to Pamela Hansford Johnson, December, 1933.

[35]Ibid.

[36]Op. cit., Ferris.

[37]Op. cit., Ferris.

[38]*Reminiscences of Childhood.*

[39]John Arlott, *Dylan Thomas and Radio,* Adelphi, Vol 30, No. 2 (1954), p. 123.

[40]Louis MacNeice, *Dylan Thomas: Memories and Appreciation, Encounter,* January, 1954, p. 12 and quoted by Bill Read, op. cit., pp. 116 - 117.

[41]Letter to Vernon Watkins, 26. August, 1946.

[42]Op. cit., Ferris, p. 225.

[43]Ibid, p. 238.

[44]Introduction to the *Letters of Vernon Watkins.*

[45]K. E. Thompson argues that Thomas was aware of musical theory. He mentions Thomas Taig's book, *Rhythm and Metre* which the Swansea poet must have read. Taig was interested in the musical effect of speech rhythms.

[46]David Daiches, *The Poetry of Dylan Thomas.*

[47]Collected Poems, *If My Head Hurt A Hair's Foot.*

[48]*Texas Quarterly IV,* Winter 1961.

[49]Collected Poems, *Altarwise by Owl-Light.*

[50]Paul Ferris suggests that Thomas was not a religious poet in the true sense of the phrase. He argues that *religion was a stage-prop of his poetry, he used its language and myth which he had learned in childhood without ever absorbing or caring much about its central beliefs. But in either case, plenty of religion was available to him in childhood, and became seeded in his brain, along with nursery rhymes and folk tales.*

[51]William T Moynihan, *The Craft and Art of Dylan Thomas.*

[52]Collected Poems, *After the Funeral.*

[53]Op. cit., Moynihan.

[54]Written answers to a student quoted by op. cit. Ferris, p. 29.

[55]Ibid. pp. 29 - 30.

[56]Letter to Pamela Hansford Johnson, December, 1933.

[57]A list of the following Swansea places mentioned includes the following:
60, Alexander Road; the Antelope Hotel, Mumbles; Bay View Hotel, Oystermouth Road; Ben Evans Department Store, Castle Bailey Street; Bethesda Welsh Chapel, Prince of Wales Road; Black Bay Inn, Killay; British Legion, 73 Mansel Street; Brynmill; Brynmill Terrace; Café Royal, High Street; Carlton Hotel, Oxford Street; Castle and Castle Street; Cefn Coed Hospital, Tycoch; Cenotaph, Mumbles Road; Chapel Street; Clevedon College; Cwmdonkin Drive; College Street; Convent School, St. James's Crescent; Cwmbwrla; Cwmdonkin; Cwmdonkin Drive, especially No. 5; Cwmdonkin Park; Cwmdonkin Terrace; Delhi Street; Dirty Black's Union Street; the Docks; Ebenezer Baptist Church, Ebenezer Street; Elysium Cinema, High Street; Empire Theatre, Oxford Street; Evening Post Offices, Castle Street; 38 Eversley Road, Sketty; Eynon's the Bakers; Fairground, Mumbles; 69, Glanbrydan Avenue; Goat Street; Grove Street; the Grammar School, Mount Pleasant; The Grove, Uplands; Hafod; Hanover Street; St. Helen's Road; High Street; High Street Arcade; Hospital, St. Helen's Road; Inkerman Street, St. Thomas; Kardomah Café, 14 Castle Street; Little Theatre, Southend, Mumbles; Llwyn y Bryn High School for Girls, Walter Road; Mackworth Hotel, High Street; Manselton; Marine Hotel, Mumbles Road; Maritime Quarter; Marks and Spencer's, Victoria Arcade; Patti Pavilion; Mermaid Hotel, Mumbles; Metropole Hotel, Wind Street: 22, Mirador Cescent, Uplands; Mirador Lane, Uplands; Mount Pleasant Hill; Mumbles; Mumbles Head; Mumbles Pier; Mumbles Road; Museum, Victoria Road; Norfolk Street; No. 10 Union Street; Oystermouth; Paraclete Congregational Church, Newton Road, Newton; Plaza Cinema, Picton Place; Promenade, Mumbles Road; Rabaiotti's Café, High Street; Recreation Ground, Mumbles Road; St. Helen's Road; St. Helen's Cricket Ground; St. Thomas, Sandfields; Swansea sands; The Slip; Singleton Park, Sketty; Sketty; Sketty Church (St. Paul's); Sketty Green; the Strand; Swansea Bay; Swansea Town AFC; Tawe, Terrace Road; The Three Lamps Hotel, Temple Street; Town Hill; Uplands; Uplands Cinema; Uplands Hotel; Upper Killay; Victoria Park; Walter Road; Woolworth's, 239 High Street and the Workhouse, Mount Pleasant.

[58]James *A Davies, Dylan Thomas's Places,* pp. 85 - 90.

[59]Letter to Countess Caetani, *Botteghe Oscure XIII* (1954).

[60]*Under Milk Wood.*

[61]Ibid.

[62]Op. cit., Moynihan.

[63]Conversation with James Laughlin. See op. cit., Ferris, p. 243.

[64]Letter to Caitlin Thomas (née Macnamara), 7th. April, 1950.

[65]Malcolm E. Gingerich, *Dylan Thomas and America* in *Dylan Thomas Remembered*, pp. 26 - 34.

[66]Letter to D. J. and Florence Thomas, 22 May, 1950.

[67]Op. cit., Gingerich.

[68]Op. cit., Ferris, pp. 317 - 318.

[69]See the portrait painted by Anthony James on p. 4 and on the back cover of this book.

BOOKLIST AND FURTHER READING

Ackerman, John. *Dylan Thomas, His LIfe and Work,* O.U.P., 1964
Welsh Dylan (Cardiff, John Jones, 1979; reproduced as Paladin paperback, Granada, 1980).

Brinnin, John Malcolm. *Dylan Thomas in America*, Dent, London, 1956.

Cox, D. B. (editor). *Dylan Thomas, A Collection of Critical Essays,* Englewood Cliffs, N.J., Prentice Hall, 1966 (paperback).

Davies, Emlyn. *Dylan Thomas Illuminations,* Swansea, Celtic Publications, 1973.

Davies, James A. *Dylan Thomas's Places,* Swansea, Christopher Davies, 1987.

Davies, Walford. *Dylan Thomas* in *Writers of Wales Series,* Cardiff, University of Wales Press, 1972.

Ferris, Paul:. *Dylan Thomas,* Hodder and Stoughton, 1977; reproduced as a Penguin paperback, 1978.

Fitzgibbon, Constantine. *The Life of Dylan Thomas,* Dent, London, 1965.

Fraser, G. S. *Dylan Thomas,* London, British Book Centre, 1957.

Gingerich, Martin E. *Dylan Thomas and America, Dylan Thomas Remembered,* Swansea, The Dylan Thomas Society, Wales Branch, 1978.

Jones, Daniel. *My Friend, Dylan Thomas,* Dent, London, 1977.

Jones, Thomas Henry. *Dylan Thomas,* Oliver and Boyd, Edinburgh, 1963.

Lewis, Min. *Laugharne and Dylan Thomas,* Dobson, 1967.

Moynihan, William T. *The Craft and Art of Dylan Thomas,* Ithaca, New York, Cornell University Press, 1966.

Read, Bill. *The Days of Dylan Thomas,* Weidenfeld and Nicholson, 1964.

Seymour, Tryntje Van Ness. *Dylan Thomas's New York,* Owings Mills, Maryland, Stemmer House, 1978.

Sinclair, Andrew. *Dylan Thomas: Poet of His People,* Michael Joseph, 1975.

Sinnock, Donald. *The Dylan Thomas Landscape,* Celtic Educational Services, Swansea, 1975.

Stead, Peter. *The Swansea of Dylan Thomas* in *Dylan Thomas Remembered,* Swansea, The Dylan Thomas Society, Wales Branch, 1978.

Tedlock, E. W. (editor). *Dylan Thomas, The Legend and the Poet: A Collection of Biographical and Critical Essays,* London, Heinemann, 1960.

Thomas, Caitlin. *Leftover Life to Kill,* Putnam, 1957.

Thompson, Kent E. *Dylan Thomas in Swansea,* unpublished Ph.D. thesis, Swansea, 1966.

Tindall, William York. *A Reader's Guide to Dylan Thomas,* New York, Farrar, Strauss and Giroux, 1962.

Watkins, Gwen. *Portrait of a Friend,* Llandysul, Gomer Press, 1983.